CALIFORNIA

AN ILLUSTRATED HISTORY

ILLUSTRATED HISTORIES FROM HIPPOCRENE

CALIFORNIA

AN ILLUSTRATED HISTORY

Robert J. Chandler

HIPPOCRENE BOOKS, INC.
New York

Unless otherwise noted, all illustrations and documents are from the author's personal collection.

ISBN 0-7818-1034-5

For information, address:
   Hippocrene Books, Inc.
   171 Madison Avenue
   New York, NY 10016

Book design and composition by Susan A. Ahlquist.

Cataloging-in-Publication data available from the Library of Congress.

Printed in the United States of America.

To my supportive wife, Susan,
already forced out of one house due to
an expanding library.

Contents

CONTENTS

Foreword

What is California? A state of the Union; a state of mind; a land of oppression; a land of dreams? These are my impressions of this mysterious region. As age and upbringing affect interpretation, I should explain that I was born during World War II and grew up as an Army brat, moving every one to three years. I have lived in the Golden State longer than any other. I have perspective from living in other places, as well as a deep attachment to this state from long stays in Southern and Northern California.

Through these pages, voices of common Californians speak from periods throughout the state's history. I chose observant people who express their feelings and make choices. Most of the selections are from letters I have collected; they exemplify their times and ring with authenticity.

History is not static; it does not end. History is not passive either. Readers with a passion for history: live vibrantly, be observant, collect, and save your incoming and outgoing letters and e-mails. The future will be grateful.

Selection, evaluation, and organization make any history impressionistic. If you do not find topics here, seek them out. An included list of books is a starting point; one also can search the Internet. I intend to leave readers with a sense of curiosity to discover more.

Robert J. Chandler
All Hallows Eve, 2003

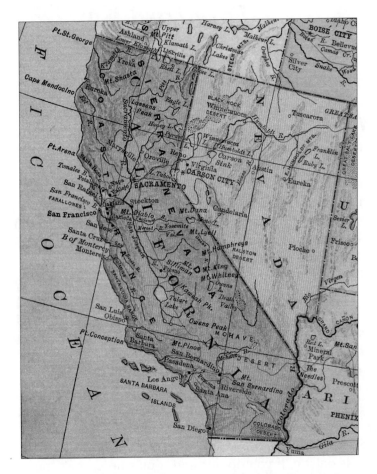

California, 1895. (Alex Everett Frye, Complete Geography *(Boston: Ginn & Company, Publishers, 1895).)*

CHAPTER I

Indians and Explorers,
Missions and Ranchos

(FROM PREHISTORY TO 1847)

California! What is this mystic land? Over geological time it can be seen as the meeting of ancient seas and crunching, mineral-rich continental plates. North to south, the Golden State stretches 800 miles; east to west, up to 250 miles. California contains roughly 160,000 square miles of land, or 100 million square acres, divided into fifty-eight irregularly shaped counties. The towering, snowy Sierra Nevada, some four hundred miles long, borders the poppy-covered Great Central Valley on one side and the state of Nevada on the other. Mount Whitney stands 14,496 feet tall, while nearby scorching Death Valley drops to 282 feet below sea level.

California is a Garden of Eden by many accounts, rich in minerals and agricultural bounty, and blessed with a pleasant climate—but not much water. Throughout the past, diversity has shaped the land's history. Some twelve thousand years ago with a receding Ice Age, Native Americans crossed in scattered groups from Asia into the New World. They came from different places at different times, but settled among one another, each group keeping its language and culture. The bountiful land provided for their needs, leading to the densest population in America. Then came European explorers, with conquerors at their heels. The eighteenth-century Spanish wished to remake the inhabitants in their own image; nineteenth-century Americans and worldwide gold-seekers cared little about the native populace. All-encompassing riches encompassed their attention.

From such beginnings modern California has emerged. The Golden State presently contains 35 million people—12 percent of the nation's population, with no single group having a majority. The population is 47 percent white, 32 percent Hispanic, 11 percent Asian, and 6 percent black. Californians together have created the world's sixth-largest economy.

THAT GOLDEN LAND

California is the third-largest state in the United States, and covering 158,693 square miles, it has the most varied landforms of any state. John S. Hittell opened the first of many editions of *Resources of California* in 1863 with these general remarks, "No other country comprises within so small a space, such various, so many, and such strongly-marked chorographical ["mapping"; current usage is "geographical"] divisions." The commercial reporter for the San Francisco *Alta California* newspaper grew poetic. "Mountains the most steep, barren, and rugged; valleys the most fertile and beautiful; deserts the most sterile; spacious bays, magnificent rivers, unparalleled waterfalls, picturesque lakes, extensive marshes, broad prairies, and dense forests—all these are hers."

Out of sea spume and fog, California's coasts loomed up as the first sight of land for European explorers. Its twelve hundred miles of coastline have three natural harbors: Humboldt in the north, San Francisco, and San Diego near the Mexican border. Only San Francisco had a great, flat expanse of developable land around its harbor.

The cliffs of Drake's Bay resemble the White Cliffs of Dover, and they are just one feature of the spectacular California coastline. (Photograph by author.)

Once ashore on solid land, settlers found reason to dispute its stability. This land of plenty can give residents plenty of shakes. From the beginning of time, the world's continents have rested on emerging, subsiding, crashing, and crunching plates, continually transforming land masses. In California, two massive continental plates grind against each other. Along the six-hundred-mile San Andreas Fault, the Pacific plate slides north, while the Northern American plate heads south, averaging two inches of movement a year. When these continental plates stick, watch out! The San Francisco earthquake on April 18, 1906, then measured at 8.25 on the Richter scale and now at 7.8 on the current earthquake energy scale, resulted from these jammed plates. With a recently confirmed epicenter in Daly City, this earthquake cracked the land for three hundred miles from San Juan Bautista to Cape Mendocino. The ground offset eighteen feet by the Point Reyes Park Headquarters; a fence split in 1906 still remains, showing the land's movement. One good thing came from the 1906 disaster: the birth of earthquake science. The ruptured ground led scientists for the first time to connect the cause of earthquakes to faults.

Furthermore, the battling continental plates are unsurpassed mountain-builders, and mountains cover half of California's land area. The coastal range, formed from uplifted young sedimentary rocks, runs along the length of the state. As these mountains form the ocean boundary of California, the great Sierra Nevada makes the eastern boundary. It is a large granite block that angles up from the west, leaving a sheer eastern face toward Nevada. The Sierra stretches about 430 miles, ranges from 40 to 80 miles wide, and covers a fifth of California. The system equals the European Alps in mass. Oak, manzanita, and pine grow up to the elevation of twenty-five hundred feet; conifers are the primary vegetation up to six thousand feet.

A tourist's 1930s decal portrays the hottest, driest place in the Western Hemisphere. Earthquakes dropped blocks of the earth's crust along fault lines while tilting up mountains. As a result, 550 square miles of Death Valley lie below sea level. During roasting days, colors bleach out, but sunrises and sunsets bring forth shadows and beautiful reds, oranges, and yellows.

From first sight, those who could write stood in awe. An overlander, fresh from crossing the plains, wrote from Placerville on August 1, 1850, to his wife in Missouri, "The sight would pay for the trouble of getting there." After passing "over snow twenty feet deep, there you view the higher peaks of the Sierra Nevada mountains standing in solid columns of hard granite pillows, as though they were stuck up there by the Almighty hand to hang the ethereal world on them. These solid mountains of stone seem to be beautifully set off with the tall cedar pine and fir tree, filled in at the roots with snow from the snow below. Beautiful streams run through full coats of grass, as growing under the snow, interspersed with beautiful flowers of every variety and hue. Then you view the red and silver lakes on either side filled with fine spotted mountain trout, around it a fine rich valley covered with fine blue grass and clover and these woods filled with deer, bear and other game so that man and horse may fare well."

Out of the Sierra run the rivers that supply California's water. The San Joaquin and Sacramento River systems that drain into the Delta and out through San Francisco Bay provide sustenance to the life of California. These two systems were a boon for gold-seekers. Marysville, Sacramento, and Stockton became supply and transportation centers. Steamers with a five-foot draft regularly sailed to Stockton; those drawing up to three feet made the journey to Sacramento, while shallow draft boats that could sail in fifteen inches of water served Marysville and Red Bluff. Today, Sacramento and Stockton handle oceangoing ships.

Other mountain ranges march north from the Sierra. The volcanic Cascade Range includes Mount Lassen (10,457 feet), which last erupted in 1917, and majestic, snow-capped Mount Shasta (14,161 feet). The Klamath Mountains, a twisted, folded knot of rock, guard the boarder into Oregon.

Half Dome looms above glaciated Yosemite Valley, with the Sierra Nevada beyond. (Photograph by Warren C. Dickerson, circa 1905.)

The great semi-arid Central Valley, blocked on the south by the Tehachapi Mountains, lies between the Sierra and Coast ranges. In the spring of 1885, one resident found the five-hundred-mile Great Central Valley, "as level as a house floor" and "with rivers interlacing it." The beauty struck him most. "All the level land at this season of the year, is carpeted with green grass, intermingled with wild flowers of all colors. It remains so, until the last of May, then it begins to dry up, and by the first of August, it is as dry as powder all about."

Tulare Lake, now evaporated due to damming of the rivers that fed it, varied year by year; in 1865 it measured thirty-five by sixty miles. Amazed, the writer declared, "I have seen the air completely alive with geese, of all kinds, just as far as I could see, in every direction, and for every day, for weeks at a time." With irrigation, this fertile valley has become the largest productive agricultural area within California. Similarly, southwest deserts receive less than three inches of rain a year. The Imperial Valley, bordering Mexico, claims the largest irrigated system in the west.

Hittell observed that California averaged 220 clear days annually, 85 cloudy ones, and only 60 that brought rain. Essentially, much of California is dry. While known for its warm Mediterranean-like climate, perfect for oranges and olives, California has seasonal rains. Winter and spring bring moisture, usually in the months between December and February.

Summers are hot, dry, and perfect for wildfires. After all, fire is very much a part of the natural cycle of renewal; seeds need it to germinate. On October 27, 2003, headlines on the Walnut Creek *Contra Costa Times* roared: "South State Inferno: Winds defy containment tactics; 300,000 acres burn. Thirteen dead; At least 850 homes destroyed; flights canceled; N[ational] F[ootball] L[eague] game moved." By November 1, the ten Southern California fires in the counties from Ventura

This photograph of a gold mine near Indio, taken by Los Angelean Warren C. Dickerson circa 1905, shows the barrenness of the Riverside County desert.

to San Diego had burned 746,000 acres. The huge Cedar Fire between Julian and San Diego became the largest recorded blaze in state history after blackening 282,000 acres. Furthermore, drought is common, regularly intensifying fire danger. Of greater import, a growing population pressures a fragile water supply.

Geographical and climatic variety brought equally diverse plants and animals. In the 1925 edition of his *A Manual of Flowering Plants of California*, University of California Botany Professor Willis Linn Jepson described 4,019 species, of which 1,416 lived only within Golden State boundaries. More troublesome were 292 hugely aggressive imports that in some areas

In 1902 the "California Limited" races past the grotesque, but intriguing, southern California Joshua Trees.

comprised 50 to 75 percent of the plant population. One of the most eye-catching was a "forty-niner," the Australian blue gum eucalyptus. Spectacular standouts among native trees include twisted Monterey cypresses clinging to the rocky coast; broadly spreading live oaks, dark green against golden hillsides; stately fog-eating coastal redwoods, gigantic Sierra sequoias, and ancient, gnarled bristlecone pines.

Newcomers found that California had an equally huge number of unknown animals. When Hubert Howe Bancroft published Titus Fey Cronise's *The Natural Wealth of California* in 1868, naturalists had found 115 species of mammals. Within a century, that number grew to 400. Foremost stood *Ursus horribilis*, the grizzly bear. This beast, ferocious when attacked,

"Ending a Life of Centuries": the original caption of this 1905 image says it all. Between 1897 and 1908, the Sanger Lumber Company logged the giant sequoias of the Converse Basin and never made a profit. Yet the disturbed and newly sunlit ground at six thousand feet favored new growth. Some young sequoias are now two feet in diameter—they have only thirty-three feet and two thousand years to go before matching the largest found in this area of the national forest.

could grow to two thousand pounds in weight, four feet high, and seven feet long. Luckily, its normal size was half that. Although the grizzly continues to live on the California state flag, by 1908 men had hunted it to extinction.

Cronise further declared that collectors had "positively ascertained" 350 species of birds, or about half of the 600 ultimately found. Eighty-five types of reptiles (eighty-four is the current tally) resided within California, predominately in hot, arid regions. Of 194 species of fish, Cronise observed, "Nearly all those found on this coast were new to naturalists in 1850." He enthused, "California is probably better supplied than any other equally populous portion of the civilized world, as regards abundance, excellence, or variety." At least 60 varieties of fish have been commercially viable.

By 1880, the state Fish Commissioners had identified 255 species of saltwater and 25 of freshwater fish. Monterey Bay, now a marine sanctuary, served as a meeting place for cold and warm water fish, and contained 130 species, including 25 of 27 types of rock cod, a food staple. Chinese fishermen hauled in five hundred pounds of the large-eyed flounder (*Hippoglossoides jordani*) from that bay every day of that year. San Francisco Bay and the rivers flowing into it yielded four thousand tons of fish in 1880, much of it salmon, while the 1880 salmon catch for all of California was five thousand tons.

Out from the Mists of Time

Out of legend, the idea of California appeared on the European consciousness. Garcia Rodriguez Ordonez de Montalvo's 1510 novel *Las Sergas de Esplandian* postulated a verdant island called California that "everywhere abounds with gold and precious stones." Naturally favored, California lay, "very close to the Terrestrial Paradise." Here Queen Calafia supposedly ruled a tribe of fierce, black Amazon archers, their arms covered in gold. When sixteenth-century Spanish explorers received rumors of riches surrounding Baja California, they assumed it was, indeed, the mythical island. Perpetuating the legend and thrown off by Baja California's long peninsula, seventeenth-century map-makers actually showed California as an island.

Native Americans knew California as it actually existed. When Spanish and English explorers located California in the sixteenth century, three hundred thousand people already called it home. Abundant food supplies allowed this large population to be sedentary hunters and gatherers—men did the former, women the latter.

Among about fifty loosely aligned cultural tribes were the Cahuillas, Chumash, Costanoans, Diegueños, Gabrielinos, Luiseños, Hoopas, Maidus, Miwoks, Modocs, Monos, Pomos, Serranos, Shastas, Washoes, Wintun, Yahis, Yanos, Yokuts, Yuroks, and Yumas. Five hundred tribelets or rancherias, as the small villages came to be called, spoke 135 different dialects from among six language families (Algonkin, Athabascan, Hokan, Penutian, Uto-Aztecan, and Yukian). Often close neighbors could not understand one another's language.

Each rancheria contained two hundred to five hundred people. A leading elder had ceremonial, but not binding authority. Each community had its own land, perhaps within a five-mile radius, with recognized boundaries beyond which none dared stray. Trespass invited death, usually in a gruesome manner, to serve as an example. Individualism did not exist in such small, close-knit societies; all together made a unified community. This California was a land without history, according to current notions. After death, no one spoke the deceased's name again, effectively erasing the past. Legends and stories, not actual events, explained the past.

13

An 1861 French magazine, Le Tour du Monde, *presents a dignified Native American hunter, though one who had adapted to European-style trousers. In his own culture, after his death no one would speak his name. Yet an inquisitive land five thousand miles away preserved his memory.*

Native Californians were hunter-gatherers. LEFT: *Here women pick up acorns, their staple food supply, while others harvest and winnow tasty grass grains.* RIGHT: *With stone tools, women used water and heat to shape fibers into world-renowned waterproof woven baskets. The bountiful land supported a large population. (Le Tour du Monde, 1861.)*

Diet was constant and consistent over large areas. Their bountiful food consisted of large and small game, fish, insects, and especially plants—nuts, seeds, leaves, stems, and roots. Highly nutritious ground and leached acorn mush was a staple—although grit from the grinding of acorns to powder in mortar holes wore down teeth. A stone outcropping in Gold Discovery State Park at Coloma exhibits numerous holes. None of the inhabitants used metal, and shining gold in Sierra stream beds held no value in their culture, either for ornament or trade. Most did not use pottery, it being too bulky, heavy, and fragile to move as tribelets migrated between summer and winter hunting grounds. Finely woven baskets, a marvel to all who have seen them, suited a variety of needs, including cooking. Agreements allowed several rancherias to share common foodstuffs in areas of plenty, such as the mountains.

In the Indian consciousness, animals and the natural world were a part of their own world. Their system of belief combined the present, the past, and myth, unifying speech, thoughts, and dreams. Out of this sense of oneness came ecological management, or shaping the land's resources to their sustainable use. Fire was the prime force used to shape the land, clearing brush from forests and encouraging tender, new, edible growth in the grasslands.

A twenty-first-century view of a "golden age" of land management is almost the counterpart of the eighteenth-century European ideal of unfettered man or "the noble savage." Of course, rancherias carried on trade, but only with what raw materials, surplus food, and manufactured goods members could carry on their backs, such as abalone shells, beads, cinnabar, obsidian, pine nuts, and salt.

EXPLORATION AND DISCOVERY

The Renaissance in Europe encouraged inquisitiveness. What of the unknown could be made known? An insatiable desire for knowledge inaugurated a European Age of Exploration in the fifteenth century. For the next four hundred years, small ocean-going ships made long, dangerous voyages into undiscovered seas, charting unknown lands. For California Indians, the option of remaining undiscovered did not exist. The only questions were, when would they encounter European explorers, and which ones would they meet first?

On September 28, 1542, Juan Rodríguez Cabrillo of Spain sailed into San Diego Bay and became the first European to see the California coast. The English sailor and buccaneer Francis Drake followed in 1579, on June 17, careening the *Golden Hind*

The King of California places his Crown of Feathers on Admiral Drakes Head

An 1815 Irish publication presents its interpretation of Sir Francis Drake's landing at Point Reyes in 1579.

to scrape sea growth from her hull, at what is now known as Drake's Bay, to the north of San Francisco. With a brass plate he secured the "right and title" of Nova Albion, or New England, for his queen. In November 1595, Sebastian Rodriguez Cermeño sought refuge in the same bay for his Manila galleon, the *San Agustin*, but on November 30, storms drove it ashore. To provide safe havens for rich ships from the Philippines that made landfall on the California coast before running down to Mexico, the Spanish king sent Sebastián Vizcaíno to chart it, which he did admirably in 1602 and 1603.

From the days of the first British settlers in the seventeenth century, the history of the east coast of North America chronicled a series of Indian wars. California's remoteness provided its inhabitants with two centuries of sanctuary from European conquest. In the late eighteenth century, though, the pace of contact quickened. Worried about a potential Russian threat from the north, the Spanish determined to secure California. In 1728, Vitus Bering sailed under the flag of Russia to find the strait that bears his name and in 1841, he explored the Alaskan coast. A wealth in furs awaited him, and in 1799, Alexander Baranov formed the Russian-American Fur Company and settled Sitka.

In 1769, the Sacred Expedition, under the commands of Captain Gaspar de Portolá and Franciscan Father Junípero Serra pushed into California; two parties entered by land from Baja California, two by sea. In late 1769, Portolá's leather-jacketed troopers discovered the apparently landlocked San Francisco Bay; the Golden Gate being exceedingly difficult to see from sea. In the meantime, at San Diego that year, Father Serra established the first of nine missions he would found before his death in 1784; his successor, Father Fermín Lasuén added another nine between 1785 and 1803. The church fathers founded the final mission at Sonoma in 1823.

Within a half-century, twenty-one missions stretched a day's distance apart along El Camino Real, the Royal Road (roughly today's Highway 101). The missions are, running south to north, San Diego de Alcalá, founded in 1769; San Luis Rey de Francia, 1798; San Juan Capistrano, 1775; San Gabriel Arcángel, 1771; San Fernando Rey de España, 1797; San Buenaventura (Ventura), 1782; Santa Bárbara, 1786; Santa Inés (at Solvang), 1804; La Purísima Concepción (five miles east of Lompoc), 1787; San Luis Obispo de Tolosa, 1772; San Miguel Arcángel, 1797; San Antonio de Padua (twenty-three miles south of King City), 1771; Nuestra Señora de la Soledad, 1791; San Carlos Borromeo de Carmelo, 1770; San Juan Bautista, 1797; Santa Cruz, 1791; Santa Clara de Asís, 1777; San José (at Fremont), 1797; San Francisco de Asís (called Mission Dolores from a nearby stream), 1776; San Rafael Arcángel, 1817; and San Francisco Solano (at Sonoma), 1823. Often, towns later grew up around the thick-walled, stone and adobe complexes with red roof tiles. Each mission included a church, artisan shops, granaries, and dormitories. Following secularization in 1834, many buildings found other uses. In the early twentieth century, widespread interest in Spanish heritage and a popular architecture known as Spanish mission style led to their restoration.

Ultimately, the Spanish priests baptized fifty-four thousand neophytes, as they called the newly converted; unconverted Indians were "gentiles." The military, for its part, established four presidios or garrison towns, south to north, at San Diego, Santa Barbara, Monterey, and San Francisco. Their duty was to round up unconverted Indians and return escaped neophytes to the missions.

Pacific Coast colonization began slowly, for Alta and Baja California were far from the Spanish center of power in Mexico City. Baja California, close to the Spanish naval base at San

A run-down Carmel Mission, founded by Father Junípero Serra in 1770, shows off an ungainly but protective roof installed in 1884. This stone building, begun in 1793, is the most beautiful of the missions and a favorite destination of tourists.

Blas, came first. As American colonists approached war with Great Britain, the pioneering *San Carlos* sailed into San Francisco Bay on August 6, 1775, to prepare the way for Captain Juan Bautista de Anza's colonists. On September 17, 1776, after a long march, families celebrated at the Presidio of San Francisco de Asís. In November of the next year, sixty-eight settlers established a *pueblo de gente de razón*, or a town for civilized people, at San José. Only eleven families inaugurated the city of Nuestra Señora la Reina de Los Angeles de Porciúncula in September 1781.

However, on the way, the unruly settlers and soldiers mistreated the Yuma Indians at the Colorado River crossing. In mid-July 1781, the Native Americans struck back at their tormentors, wiping out two missions, closing Anza's overland route from Mexico, and delaying the founding of the pueblo. New settlers continued to arrive, however, and by 1821, "Californios," or those born in Alta California, numbered thirty-three hundred.

As missions, presidios, and pueblos struggled to survive, the "Russian threat" materialized early in the nineteenth century. Otter hunters appeared in California in 1803, but the home base at Sitka experienced crisis. While fur-bearing animals abounded in plenty, food did not. When the czar's chamberlain, Count Nikolai Petrovich Rezanov, arrived on an inspection trip in 1805, he found mass starvation. On March 8, 1806, he sailed into San Francisco harbor in search of supplies. A whirlwind courtship of Doña Concepción Argüello, daughter of the presidio commander, overcame Spanish hostility and gained him the needed foodstuffs. Rezanov departed after two months on May 8. His early death in Russia, and her alleged unrequited love became a literary legend by the 1870s.

In 1812, Governor Ivan Koskov arrived, ignored Spanish claims, and brazenly built Fort Ross in Sonoma County, with about two hundred Russians and Kodiak Indians. Russian warehouses and shipbuilding sprouted at Bodega, while hunters based on the Farralone Islands off the Golden Gate killed up to fifty thousand gulls a year, plus sea lions as food for the Aleuts. These natives, for their part, were unparalleled pelt hunters and by the 1820s had cleaned out the otters from San Francisco Bay and along much of the coast. Fort Ross also supplied food for Sitka, which the Russians gained by trade rather than farming or raising stock.

Economics and international politics ended the settlement. Spanish and Mexican governors tolerated, but never recognized, the Russian usurpations of their land and issued land grants to block eastward expansion. Furthermore, in 1824, U.S. Secretary of State John Quincy Adams negotiated a treaty by which Russia gave up claims south of latitude 54°40' north, and the Americans began to increase pressure. By the late 1830s, Fort Ross ate money rather than producing it. As an alternative, the fur company negotiated with the British Hudson's Bay Company to supply Sitka from Oregon. In 1841, the Russians withdrew, selling what they could not take away to John Sutter in Sacramento.

CULTURAL CLASH

With the arrival of Europeans, new diseases, plants, and animals worked to upset California's ecological balance, while Spanish colonists—whites, Christianized Indians, blacks, and people of mixed background—unleashed new cultural forces. Spaniards were indeed men with a mission. Their unwavering view of the world included an all-powerful God, the divine right of kings, and the ranking of social classes within an orderly world. They set to work rounding up local peoples and

22

confining them to the missions, for Indians would be made Spanish. Of course, the process was easy in theory but impossible to produce.

Missions were meant to be only temporary homes for the native inhabitants. There, Indians would gain everlasting life through the salvation of their souls. Knowledge of crafts and agriculture would make them self-sufficient and able to support a larger population of useful people. Ultimately, formerly nomadic Indians cultivated ten thousand acres, annually producing one hundred thousand bushels of wheat and corn. They herded sixty thousand horses, three hundred thousand hogs, sheep, and goats, and four hundred thousand cattle.

In practice, things worked differently. Spanish settlers, imbued with Enlightenment ideals of reason, were the *gente de razón*. On the other hand, Indians, though human, were *sin razón*, or without reason. The colonists considered them to be at a lower level, childlike, governed by instinct, not rational thought. A Russian visitor in 1829 saw the abundance of the land and felt the mild climate, and remarked that among such bounty, the Indian had "no reason for exerting his intellectual capacities." Ironically, the next wave of conquerors would apply the same logic to the Californios.

Too often, the shock of disrupted lives, new foods, and virulent diseases led mission neophytes to infertility and death—yet missions were better than the huge private cattle ranchos, whose owners felt no social duties. Yet, even the ranchos were better than the later Gold Rush treatment of native inhabitants. Venereal diseases, especially syphilis, wrecked havoc, while epidemics of malaria occurred in 1833, and smallpox broke out in 1837 and 1838. Culturally, the hunter-gatherers living at the missions could not comprehend farming, or the rationale for learning the skills of artisans. Even a sense of time was alien.

However, over time Indians adeptly learned new crafts, the Spanish language, and horseback riding. They worked to blend their traditional life with the new, often rebelled, sometimes returned, and created new ways to survive. From 1828 to 1829, Estanislao, a San Jose neophyte, led a band of one thousand rebels, built elaborate fortifications, held off three Mexican attacking forces, and later found forgiveness at the mission. During the next decade, escaped neophytes joined with unconquered Native Americans to lead continuous horse raids along the Central Valley frontier. Still, the Indian population dropped to half pre-contact numbers.

Provincial government, though, remained feeble, whether under Spain or Mexico. Distance from the seats of power was long, while settlers, money, supplies, and even interest were short. In 1821, Mexico wrested its independence from Spain, and could have taught its more powerful neighboring republic to the north lessons in civil rights. While the U.S. Constitution legalized slavery, the Mexican declaration of independence stated, "All the inhabitants of New Spain, without distinction, whether European, African, or Indian, are citizens of the Monarchy, with a right to be employed in any post, according to their merits and virtues." Instability, factional fighting, and strained resources limited what Mexico City could do for its distant, sparsely settled province. Governors came and went with little effect on the landed families. California actually had little use for provincial government. On the local level, *Alcaldes*, the chief town officials, administered justice in a manner suited to the resolution of conflicts in a small community, without confrontation or bad feelings between winners and losers.

In Spanish California, missions became basic business units. After fulfilling their own needs, they then supplied food and contract laborers to the presidios, and a variety of trade goods for all, such as saddles, bridles, tack, wool blankets,

A nineteenth-century Indian plows fields around the Santa Barbara Mission, founded 1786, as his family did before him. Native American labor built "The Queen of the Missions" between 1820 and 1834. Besides livestock husbandry and agriculture, the missions taught basic carpentry and blacksmithing skills, in the attempt to turn nomadic Native Americans into settled European peasants. The Mexican Government secularized the missions in 1834.

wine, and brandy. The Franciscan fathers were able merchants who bought in bulk from Yankee traders and local producers, extended credit and goods among the other missions, and promptly paid their bills. Theirs was a self-sufficient economy, existing without outside investment. The missions and ranchos produced grains, hides, and tallow for export. Grazing cattle, however, caused an ecological disaster as they stripped hills of native vegetation.

COMMERCE OPENS DOORS

When the trading of cowhides to Boston began in 1822, ship captains looked to the missions for supplies. From 1828 on, the firm of John Bryant, William Sturgis & Company dominated this business until a crash in hide prices during 1845 closed this economic enterprise. Californios had no factories and yearned for manufactured goods, while New England shoe-makers needed good hides. Merchants emerged to handle these transactions. In 1827, John Temple and George Rice opened the first store in Los Angeles. The medium of exchange became "California Bank Notes," cowhides worth $2 cash. In Boston, each hide brought $2.75, enough profit to justify a three-year voyage. Southern California supplied most of the hides. Some 40 percent came out of San Pedro, the port for the City of Angels.

Richard Henry Dana captured the spirit of this trade and of the grand rancho families in 1830s California. One day in early May 1835, as Dana recounted in his popular *Two Years before the Mast* (1840), he stood on a four-hundred foot cliff pitching hides for men below to catch and load aboard ship. "As they were all large, stiff, and doubled, like the cover of a book, the wind took them, and they swayed and eddied about, plunging and rising in the air." He continued, "As they came to ground, the men below picked them up, and taking them on their heads, walked off with them to the boat. This was the romance of hide-droghing!"

With adventurers like Dana, a diverse population developed gradually. The world's ships came visiting; fur trapper Jedediah Smith arrived in 1826; and in 1841, John Bidwell led the first overland pioneer train from Missouri. California saw representatives from the Aleutian Islands, Hawaii, China, Europe, New England, and most places in between. "What California lacks is workers," Frenchman Auguste Duhaut-Cilly penned in 1827.

As this son of France observed on his trading voyage, opportunities for skilled artisans abounded. Many of the newcomers brought skills unknown in agrarian California. Of special importance in the 1820s were carpentry and shipbuilding, and in 1843, Irishman Jasper O'Farrell became the first professional surveyor in Alta California. To participate in society, immigrants applied for Mexican citizenship, including conversion to Catholicism, and learned Spanish. The fortunate married into the landed gentry.

On August 9, 1834, Governor José Figueroa, a respected administrator, began secularizing the missions, following a decree of the Mexican Congress a year previously. Not only did politicians fear the power of the Catholic Church, but its rich properties fueled greed. In practice, land passed into private hands through seven hundred government grants, and the Indians had to fend for themselves. Many in effect became peons, bound to the landed estates. The life of the aristocratic grantees gave rise to the pastoral legend of Old Spanish California, as portrayed in *Zorro*.

27

CONQUEST BY THE UNITED STATES

In the meantime, word spread that California held plenty of good land, owned by the ignorant and idle Mexicans—characterizations reminiscent of Californio opinions of the Indians—waiting for an energetic people to develop it. Thomas Jefferson Farnham declared in 1846, "the Californians are an imbecile, pusillanimous race of men, and unfit to control the destinies of that beautiful country."

Through the 1840s, European powers eyed California as a tempting prize, though Russia had dropped out. The otter hunters departed Fort Ross in 1839 and sold the property to Captain John Sutter. This Swiss adventurer maintained a border fort at the future site of Sacramento to protect the frontier. The British and French and above all, the United States, manifested eager interest. The fledgling American republic believed it had the God-given "Manifest Destiny" to spread from ocean to ocean, even though current settlement only reached the Missouri River. In 1842, acting on rumors of hostilities, Navy Commodore Thomas Jones mistakenly captured the provincial Mexican capital at Monterey. Then in 1846, a Texas-Mexican border dispute erupted into war, and the United States took the opportunity to seize what we call the Southwest: Texas, New Mexico, Arizona, and Alta California.

During the war, American settlers north of San Francisco feared Mexican authorities would expel them. With the covert support of Army topographical engineer John Charles Frémont, on June 14, 1846, a group of thirty-four captured Sonoma and created the short-lived Bear Flag Republic. Although the original animal resembled a pig more than a grizzly bear, in 1911, it became the California state flag. The current design dates from 1953.

John Charles Frémont (1830–1890) often stood in the right place at the right time—but could not succeed. While he was on hand for the conquest of California, others took charge; when made the first California senator, he drew the short term; and floating a purchased land grant to cover the fabulously wealthy Mariposa mines, Frémont watched a fortune slip by. (C.W. Upham, Life, Explorations, and Public Services of John Charles Fremont *(Boston: Ticknor and Fields, 1856).)*

American military forces were also ready to seize California. Under orders to prevent the British capture of California in case the United States and Mexico went to war, Commodore John Sloat landed at Monterey on July 7, 1846. Meantime, Captain John Montgomery of the sloop of war *Portsmouth* came ashore at San Francisco on July 9, soon giving the name of his ship to the main plaza, while his own graced the commercial thoroughfare. The Stars and Stripes flew above both towns, and California, a land inhabited by fifteen thousand Californios and one hundred and fifty thousand Indians was under U.S. military rule.

Miscues, stupidity, and oppression in particular by glory-seeking Navy Commodore Robert F. Stockton and erratic Marine Major Archibald H. Gillespie led Californios to revolt and teach American troopers just how sharp long lances could be. General José Maria Flores recaptured Los Angeles from the tyrannical Gillespie on September 30, 1846, but his Californios could not change the result.

On January 13, 1847, General Andrés Pico, victor on December 6, 1846, over General Stephen Watts Kearny's dragoons at San Pasqual (east of Escondido, San Diego County), surrendered to Frémont at Campo de Cahuenga, North Hollywood, Los Angeles. The four-month insurrection ended. Three months later, the nine hundred and fifty men of Colonel Jonathan D. Stevenson's New York regiment arrived as colonizers, and land speculators quickly dominated the life of the small village of Yerba Buena, just recently renamed San Francisco.

CHAPTER II

From Gold Rush to Railroad:
A Man with a Hunch
Changes History
(1847–1870)

In 1834, John Augustus Sutter left his family in Switzerland to seek his fortune. New York, Santa Fe, Oregon, Honolulu, and Sitka saw him before he arrived in Mexican California in 1839. He would build an agricultural empire and guard the frontier on a huge eleven-square-league grant from the governor, some forty-eight thousand acres.

The American conquest changed little at New Helvetia, Sutter's settlement, which became Sacramento. Sutter had vast farms, Indian laborers to work them, and skilled craftsmen. Western-bound settlers arriving overland always stopped to share his legendary hospitality and praise his accomplishments. Sutter needed little more, but he realized that growing settlement had increased the demand for milled lumber. Boards made taller and more elegant houses than logs or adobe, and certainly were better for flooring.

While American and Mexican negotiators settled the late hostilities through the Treaty of Guadalupe Hidalgo, signed on February 2, 1848, and ratified on May 30, Captain Sutter in August 1847 sent a party under James Marshall forty-eight miles into the foothills of the Sierra mountains to build a saw

Flags and laundry wave among the white tents of gold seekers encamped on San Francisco's verdant Telegraph Hill. On top, the 1850 semaphore station announces the arrival of an American sloop of war. (Anonymous painting courtesy of Wells Fargo.)

mill along the American River. While there, the practical and inventive Marshall had a hunch. He had noticed quartz outcroppings along the riverbed, and he knew that on March 7, 1842, ranchero Francisco Lopez, while looking for wild onions, had found gold at Southern California's Placerita Canyon.

To gain water power for the undershot mill, Marshall's party dug the tail race during the day, and let the force of the river scour this canal at night. Figuring that the force of water would treat the ditch as a giant sluice box, carrying away debris and exposing bedrock, Marshall ordered the headgate closed and caulked. On January 24, 1848, James Marshall walked the ditch, checking crevices. Suddenly came the cry, "Hey, boys, by God, I believe I've found a gold mine!" He had.

GOLD-SEEKING ENTREPRENEURS SET PATTERNS FOR A STATE

In order to make history, a person must do more than just discover, do, or invent something. Whatever it is needs to be publicized to make certain everyone hears about it. Sam Brannan told Californians about Marshall's gold, while President James K. Polk told America and the world.

Lackadaisical interest greeted the news of Marshall's discovery until late spring of 1848. On May 10, adventurer and speculator Sam Brannan returned to San Francisco from the gold mines. "Gold! Gold! Gold from the American River," Brannan shouted from Portsmouth Square, waving aloft his hat in one hand and a bottle of gold dust in the other. His news quickly depopulated the Bay City, as citizens rushed to the mountains to find their own fortunes. At the end of the summer, Mrs. Ann Eliza Brannan (Sam's wife) exclaimed, "Now is the time for making money." She had just obtained $500 sewing and importing clothing for the newcomers.

On December 5, 1848, President James K. Polk presented his fourth annual message to Congress. Relying on Governor Mason's "authentic report"—accompanied by 15.75 pounds of gold, the President confirmed the "extraordinary character" of the golden abundance. He added further believability to the stories of gold just lying around waiting to be picked up. "Nearly the whole of the male population of the country has gone to the gold districts." The federal government placed no restrictions or taxes upon mining and left gold-seekers to make their own regulations. Then, the world rushed in.

Why did so many answer the call? Late in the Gold Rush, one brother wrote from Battle Creek, Michigan, on March 11, 1852, to another in Jackson, California. "I have not much hopes of ever getting out of debt, although perhaps I may manage to get along and earn a mean kind of living for my family a few years longer." California was the new hope for settlers, as he added: "Everyone who can raise money enough to take them there are going." A year later, a miner in Coyoteville echoed this optimism, "This is a great country this. A man can dig his money himself."

So they came, from the far ends of the earth by ship across the broad Pacific, or around treacherous, stormy Cape Horn— a three- to six-month trip from the eastern seaboard. Others steamed along the month-long mail route from New York to Aspinwall (now Colon), crossed the disease-infested jungle of the Panama Isthmus, and again boarded a mail steamer for San Francisco.

Others traveled by land. They started from St. Louis, Missouri, and spent the spring and summer crossing the broad prairies, the Rocky Mountains, the waterless deserts of Nevada, and finally, the high Sierra. This journey had to be accomplished before cruel winter set in, or the settlers would be trapped like the Donner Party in 1846, which famously resorted to cannibalism before all its members perished.

Their goal was to strike it rich and go home wealthy. Most felt as did Ann Eliza Brannan in September 1848: "We would never think of settling here for life." Money was their single-minded pursuit. One "forty-niner" reflected in January 1850: "As it is, there are only three things to interest us: Gold, Provisions, and Indians. We are constantly hearing reports of new diggings and rich leads, in which from two to four ounces [$32–64] may be made a day, but then provisions cost there perhaps $5 a pound and about one day in seven must be spent at fighting the Indians."

COLD, WET, AND LONELY, GAMBLING FOR FORTUNE

Mining was a lonely job, as miners joined with a few companions and constantly sought new strikes. Men often worked with others from their hometowns or states to gain a sense of community. With no government-sponsored social services, many found emotional solace, communal companionship, and financial relief in fraternal organizations, such as the Masons, Odd Fellows, and the most boisterous of all, E Clampus Vitus, which humorously summed up its mission—"To take care of the widows and orphans—particularly the widows."

Mining became romantic only after the fact, as men looked back on "the days of old, the days of gold, the days of '49." At the time, it was everything but glamorous. Miners stood in cold streams, constantly digging, blistering hands, and working long hours. They embarked on great engineering efforts, diverting rivers to penetrate the river gravels to where gold, seven times heavier than quartz, sank to bedrock. One

A single miner swirled paydirt in a pan hoping for a trace of color; two or more used a rocker or cradle. Here one Chinese miner rocks the cradle, a second dumps debris from another rocker, two others carry the source of their hopes, and the fifth digs. (Le Tour du Monde, 1861.)

miner wrote from the Tuolumne River in September 1851, "My hopes have been great. I am now damming the rivers again. If the wet season don't set in soon I will make money—if it does [washing everything away], I am ruined again."

Another miner remarked from Amador County in July 1853, "The average wage here is about $3 a day. Some days we take out $15 or $20 and other days a good deal less." North of him, a Sierra county miner stated, "I can earn a living much easier here than in New England," and he stayed on. In 1864, a miner who had rushed to barren Santa Catalina Island, answered in reply to whether he had found his "pile" of treasure, "A pile of hills was the pile I found."

For some miners, living in California became a de facto divorce. Through the early 1850s, William Coruth wrote his wife and four children in Vermont from the southern mines. The rawness of life and crudeness of furnishings comes through. "Wife, I am setting beside a good fire writing this letter to you, and I am also sitting on a box, writing on a good table of my own making. I have a candlestick on the table of my own make. I am going to save some pretty specimens for all of my children and the prettiest of all for you, wife."

He and a brother built themselves a house "thirteen feet square inside," and he bragged on January 8, 1855, "Our house looks as neat as any parlor, tonight." Coruth also became a good cook, and a traveling butcher brought by fresh beef and pork. "Wife, I made a good lot of mince meat the other evening. I had a tin pan about full when I had got all the fixings in it. It was made of fresh beef, fresh pork, and deer meat. There are five partners of us in the five claims. I gave all of my partners one pie apiece and they all said it was first rate. They said that I could beat any woman making mince pies." Ten years later, Coruth still faithfully wrote his wife from the land of gold.

Other miners led less refined lives. A gold-seeker in Yuba County described his gourmet eating. Available were "all kinds of provisions, that is, beans. We generally get them for a variety twenty-one times a week." A county neighbor let his appearance go. "I shave every week or two" he said. A Sierra County miner summed up his experience in 1863: "You know when a fellow is through with his day's work he has got to bake a loaf or wash the dishes or cut wood or do something or else there will be a rough night in the shack. And when Sunday comes, there is a half dozen dirty shirts to wash or else go to town for some grub."

Since most buildings were wooden frames with canvas room partitions and ceilings, fire was a constant threat. Charles T. Blake, Wells, Fargo & Co.'s agent at Michigan Bluff, Placer County, found his routine of shipping and receiving gold, checks, packages, and letters interrupted on the afternoon of July 29, 1857: "About four o'clock P.M. as I was washing my hands, I heard a man say 'Fire,' in a sort of inquiring tone, and looking out the window saw the fire coming. I gave the alarm." Within three minutes, "the whole office was wrapped in flames." However, Blake exhibited the enterprising California spirit. "By five o'clock the fire had subsided so that man could work his way down the street," and the busy Blake acted, for "by half-past five I had a sign painted and we opened office in Shawl's store." Reconstruction often brought brick buildings with green and black iron fire shutters.

Once miners found gold, what did they do with it? Neither gold dust nor gold bars were legal tender. As a commodity, gold dust passed at $16 a troy ounce in 1848, and $17.25 in 1852. The standard for weighing precious metals is still the troy system. A troy ounce has 480 grains compared to an ordinary avoirdupois ounce of 437.5 grains. Miners had to get dust exchanged for legal tender gold coins, and the many express companies performed this needed service. They safely and speedily sent raw gold to San Francisco's private assayers and branch mint and returned with coins.

Auburn, east of Sacramento and the county seat of Placer County, sat at a stagecoach crossing, allowing Wells Fargo's agent, John Q. Jackson, to purchase almost $200,000 in gold dust monthly, weighing about eight hundred pounds. "When we make a shipment," he wrote on September 15, 1854, "'tis frequently 100 to 150 pounds, about as much as one likes to shoulder to and from the stages." Did he fear robbers? No. "As a friend, counselor and safeguard," he had a 128-pound bulldog, who was "devoted to his business."

*The object all miners sought: This 201-troy ounce nugget (about four-
teen pounds or six kilograms) formed in crevices of quartz at Spanish
Dry Diggings, El Dorado County. Discovered in 1865, and bought by
Frenchman Jules Fricot, it amazed crowds at the 1867 Paris World's
Fair, just as today its eighteen inches (forty-five centimeters) enthrall
visitors to the Mariposa County Fair Grounds.*

*In the mid-1850s, Californians began to cast gold dust into bars for
easier shipping, and the Fricot Nugget rests on three of these. The large
center bar is about 3.5 inches [nine centimeters] long and weighs one
hundred troy ounces. The name of an 1866 San Francisco assayer is
cast on each bar: from left to right they are John G. Kellogg, John Hew-
ston & Co.; Henry Hentsch & Francis Berton; and Augustus P. Molitor.*

By 1854, the output of placer gold, found in stream bed gravels, dropped sharply. The Gold Rush was over, and miners needed capital to mine gold still imbedded in hard quartz rock or to blast away compacted gravel hillsides with huge hydraulic nozzles. Miners now often worked for wages—$4 a day became standard pay—but remained footloose and migratory within California. Suddenly, a string of new gold discoveries drew off many. In the spring of 1858, the Fraser River gold "fever" raged through California, sending adventurers to British Columbia.

In the next year, the first of many rushes to Nevada began. The prominent Sacramento Bank of D.O. Mills & Co. wrote an upstate New York customer on December 17, 1859: "The Washoe diggings [of Virginia City] are a matter of fact." The Comstock Lode silver mines indeed were "rich, very rich." Almost as an afterthought he added that "great excitement" erupted throughout the city. "There are piles of silver," the banker proclaimed a month later, all of which he expected "will be found next summer."

In 1861 and 1862, eastern Oregon, Washington, and Idaho became favored destinations, and Arizona, Utah, and Montana followed. In 1860, 38 percent of California's laborers mined; by 1870 only 15 percent were miners and a larger number of placer miners were Chinese.

Forming Social Order

California, of course, was more than one huge gold mine. It appeared on the world scene as a tangled sociological knot with its ethnically mixed population. Government carried on with little help from Congress, which could not be bothered to establish a territorial government. From July 7, 1846, until

December 20, 1849, five military officers ruled the conquered province. In particular, Colonel Richard B. Mason and General Bennett Riley eased the transition into civil government.

Riley called a constitutional convention in August 1849, and then stepped aside when Californians formed their new government. California's population grew so quickly that it escaped a territorial period and in 1850, it was as a state that California applied to Congress for direct admission into the Union.

Similar Congressional slowness appeared regarding other things Californians needed immediately. The foremost of these was money. Although President Polk asked Congress to establish a branch mint in December 1848, it did not open in San Francisco until April 1854, and did not come into full operation until 1856. In the meantime, Californians made their own gold coins, ranging in value from 25 cents to $50.

Californians also created a private service for letter delivery. In 1849, "expressmen" began taking letters that the semi-monthly mail steamers delivered to San Francisco or then by riverboats to the supply centers of Marysville, Sacramento, and Stockton, to customers in the remote regions of the mining country. On return trips, they carried gold and outgoing letters, and through the 1860s, they handled most of the mail within California. Wells, Fargo & Co. finally discontinued its letter express in 1895.

By 1852, the new state had 250,000 people, and there were at least 435,000 by 1860. To expand upon the 1860 census figures, 27 percent of Californians were born in the Northeast and Midwest, 11 percent hailed from the Southern states, and 10 percent were California-born. Others came from Europe: the population was 9 percent Irish, 6 percent British, 6 percent German, 2 percent French, and 3 percent from other countries. In all, 26 percent of California residents were European-born, and 37 percent were foreign-born, including 11 percent Chinese. The indigenous

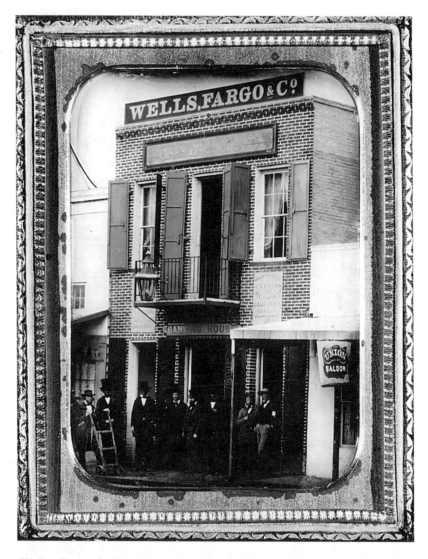

Wells, Fargo & Co.'s first office at 424 Montgomery Street, San Francisco. Opening on July 13, 1852, the express and banking firm also brought gold to market and, in lieu of poor government services, delivered letters. Wells Fargo Bank is the oldest in the West, and it maintains a free museum at 420 Montgomery Street displaying its legendary past. (Courtesy of Wells Fargo.)

Indians contributed 8 percent, Californios and other Latinos made up 6 percent, and African Americans comprised 1 percent of the population. Though women kept arriving slowly, the ratio in 1860 was still six men to every woman.

A San Franciscan observed in September 1851: "There is a certain 'free and easy' manner that [one] obtains in society—a commingling of the fashions, habits and economy, of the people here, from every State in the Union and almost every nation on the globe." In 1860, the foreign-born comprised between one third and one half of the residents in each of fifteen counties, including San Francisco, and ten of the fifteen mining counties. How would society assimilate people from so many diverse cultures, in a land where few planned to settle permanently?

In practice, the majority trampled the rights of those deemed too dissimilar, and grudgingly made accommodations for others. More often than not, settlers shot Indians on sight, and ignored Californios, or Native Californians, and other Spanish-speakers from Mexico, Chile, and elsewhere, except in sparsely settled, ranching Southern California, where they formed the majority. The populace reluctantly, and sometimes with violence, tolerated blacks and Chinese, but deprived them of all legal rights. The 1860s would bring legal reform.

New Englanders dominated culture—literature, education, and religion, while Southerners controlled politics. Most from the South were firmly wedded to belief in white supremacy, the institution of slavery, and the principle of state sovereignty. Among the foreign-born, the French refused to renounce allegiance to Emperor Napoleon III and did not become citizens, while the Irish continually fought the stereotype of the drunken, brawling Irishman. Germans celebrated Sundays with music, dancing, theater performances, and drinking. These practices shocked most settlers from the Northeast. For more

43

than thirty years, Germans battled laws requiring businesses to close on Sundays. Similarly, Jewish merchants who observed their Sabbath on Saturday saw no reason why they should shut their stores on Sunday. In 1861, Germans noisily demonstrated outside the home of a San Francisco police judge who upheld the Sunday Law.

IN THIS GARDEN OF EDEN, VIOLENCE IS COMMON

In a land where most saw themselves as sojourners temporarily thrust among strangers, violence became all too common. Today, an average rate of murder in the United States is 10 killings per 100,000 people; in 1997, Los Angeles had 33 murders per 100,000; in 2002, "murder capital" Washington, D.C. tallied 45 per 100,000. Yet these rates are minimal in comparison with those of California in the mid-nineteenth century. In the years 1850 and 1851, the Hispanic pueblo of Los Angeles saw 31 murders per 2,500 people, or 1,240 per 100,000, and through much of that decade, even pastoral Monterey County's rate stood at 333 killings per 100,000.

Nevada and Tuolumne Counties in the gold country averaged 81 and 110 per 100,000 respectively over several years in the 1850s, while more peaceful San Francisco had a mere 47 per 100,000. Reported murders alone gave the entire state in 1854 and 1855 a ratio of 180 per 100,000. How did this compare with East Coast homicide rates? Boston, Philadelphia, and New York City rates were 3 per 100,000. No wonder gold-seekers complained of crime. In an era when society expected a man to "kill his own snakes," rather than turning matters over to elected or appointed officials, miners and merchants often took the law into their own hands. Ethnicity and race played a strong role in their selection of targets.

In the 1850s a high percentage of outlaws were Californios or Mexicans, who had many legitimate grievances after being on the losing side in the recent war. However, as they were indiscriminate in killing and looting, greed was their motivation, not social justice. The best-known gang of outlaws was a geographically wide-ranging band composed of teenagers and men in their early twenties. Its leader was Claudio Feliz, and later his brother-in-law, Joaquin Murietta. Between December 1850 and March 1853, the gang killed some fifty men.

In December 1850, Claudio Feliz and his gang robbed the still-standing stone house of Contra Costa County pioneer John Marsh, killing one American. Ten days later they robbed and brutally murdered three American ranchers near San Jose. The next summer in 1851, brothers Claudio, Jesus, and Reyes Feliz with Joaquin Murietta looted through the southern and then the northern mines.

To the north in Yuba County in November 1851, the gang robbed and murdered another five men. The next year, the number of killings increased. Victims were often lassoed from horses and wagons and then stabbed to death. They included Latinos, blacks, and Chinese, as well as Americans and Europeans. However, their robbery of a Californio in Monterey County led to a battle with a posse in September 1852 that ended the career and life of Claudio Feliz.

Murietta then took charge of the band, heading to San Gabriel, near Los Angeles, where he shot Judge Joshua Bean on November 7, 1852. Shortly thereafter, vigilantes hanged Reyes Feliz for complicity. In January 1853, Joaquin Murietta's band then engaged in a legendary killing spree that ran through March. In a continuous string of robberies in Calaveras, Amador, and Mariposa counties, they killed at least ten Americans, five Frenchmen, and eleven Chinese.

Gold Rush artist Charles Christian Nahl's drawing captured the defiance of outlaw Joaquin Murietta. Though romanticized, Murietta murdered and robbed Californians of all ethnicities and backgrounds until his 1853 death. No Robin Hood-style "social banditry" was to be found here.

The legislature responded in May 1853, placing Captain Henry Love in charge of twenty chosen California Rangers. On July 10, 1853, at Mission San Jose (today's Fremont), Love captured Jesus Feliz, the last of the bandit brothers, who offered to trade Murietta's location for his freedom.

The Rangers and Murietta met on July 25, 1853, at Cantua Creek, near Coalinga in Fresno County, and Joaquin Murietta died. To obtain the bounty, Love severed and pickled Joaquin's head and placed it on display. It survived in a museum until the 1906 San Francisco earthquake. Jesus Feliz, the surviving brother, "went straight," married, settled down, and died in Bakersfield about 1910. The memory of the gang survived in local mythology.

SOCIAL STRATIFICATION AND DISCRIMINATION

On April 13, 1850, the first legislature succumbed to Mexican War jingoism and anti-foreign sentiment by passing a law euphemistically called, "An Act for the better regulation of the Mines, and the government of Foreign Miners." This law taxed aliens $20 a month, or a week's wages. It so depopulated the southern mines of their fifteen thousand Latino workers that merchants clamored for its repeal. After only eleven months, on March 14, 1851, the legislature repealed the act, and the governor announced that fact in English, French, and Spanish. The San Francisco *Alta California* rejoiced: "It was a very unfortunate enactment, [in] violation of private rights, constitutional guarantees, our national policy, considerations of expediency, and the professions which we have made to the struggling and oppressed world, for more than half a century."

On March 30, 1853, the legislature returned to the subject, setting the tax at a more reasonable $4 a month, a day's

47

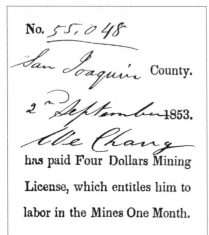

No. *55,048*

San Joaquin County.

2nd September 1853.

We Chang

has paid Four Dollars Mining License, which entitles him to labor in the Mines One Month.

From 1853 to 1871, a Foreign Miners' Tax encouraged foreigners to become voters. Set at one day's wage, the fee was not onerous but it was discriminatory. After 1860, tax collectors applied this prime source of county funding exclusively to the Chinese, who legally could not become citizens. Yet, the law did give aliens the right to mine, nullifying any local mining regulations to the contrary. This stub verifies that We Chang could mine for the month of September 1853 in San Joaquin County.

wage, and encouraging the foreign-born to become citizens. The burden of the tax fell on those who would not become citizens, such as the French, and those who could not become citizens, the Chinese. Yet, the law did give these foreigners a legal right to "labor in the Mines," which local mining laws could not deny. By the 1860s, the generally exhausted California placer mines were in the hands of the Chinese, and the foreign miners tax supplied the revenue to run county governments. In January 1871, the federal circuit court struck down this hated tax.

Californios suffered grievously from "white collar" crime, rather than violent acts of despolation. The greatest amount of contention arose over some eight hundred Spanish and Mexican land grants that governors made to private individuals before the American conquest. The U.S. Government promised to protect them under the 1848 Treaty of Guadalupe Hidalgo. In 1851, Congressionally established procedure led to "delay upon delay," as one land-use attorney remarked, and the rugged

48

journey of a land claim through the travails of the Land Commission, the District Court, and the U.S. Supreme Court sometimes took twenty years. Interjected with politics and favoritism, most claims ended up in the hands of attorneys, as well as those with the greatest stamina and deepest pockets. Enforcement of title became an additional burden, as grantees floated boundaries to take in settler improvements, while squatters usurped the best land of grants. On August 14, 1850, Sacramento settlers objecting to John Sutter's land claims shot the sheriff and badly wounded the mayor. On several occasions through the 1850s and 1860s, the governor called out troops to remove squatters.

The science of the day—since soundly repudiated—and popular opinion held that people of color were inferior, and the first state legislature undertook to set them apart. "No black or mulatto person, or Indian, shall be permitted to give evidence in favor of, or against, any white person," declared the Golden State's first criminal statute. The next legislature extended the ban to civil suits, and in 1854, the state supreme court, in the absence of legislative action, included Chinese. White men and women, the court concluded, must be "shielded from the testimony of the degraded and demoralized caste."

NATIVE AMERICANS

The heaviest blow fell upon the Native Americans. One half-literate miner wrote home in May 1854, "We wer out last Sunday, a diger ["diggers," a contemptuous term for Native Americans] hunting and we kild 36 and taken 7 priserners, and we wer but five men." He added, "so you se that we are pretty good after them." More horrifying, he accused them of no crime.

49

Neither the state nor the federal government had the desire, time, energy, or money to incorporate a rapidly shrinking population of Indians into the majority society. In 1852, the federal government made a good-faith attempt to negotiate eighteen treaties and set apart one-seventh of the state for reservations. However, no California congressman wished to commit political suicide by supporting the treaties, and the U.S. Senate killed them in secret session. In mid-1850s, the federal government did establish several poorly administered reservations, all under the protection of the regular army. However, it had few men, spread thin, and ill-suited to fight against such an elusive foe. Furthermore, the army, to its everlasting credit, worked to protect Indians from settler excesses.

The state occasionally, and in a cumbersome fashion, called out militia units to fight Indian wars. No county official, though, had any legal duty to protect its residents from marauders. Small ranchers and farmers barely making a livelihood took matters into their own hands. Local companies formed and equipped by neighbors took care of Indians in their own way—to detriment of the Native Americans. Raids came to be partially financed by the sale of Indian children as slaves. Girls brought the highest fees.

During the Civil War, the California Volunteers provided the manpower to finally crush Indian resistance. Due to a combination of disease, disruption of food sources, and murder, the Native American population dropped from 150,000 in 1848 to 30,000 in 1870.

Individually, Indians could survive in white society. In July 1851, an Indian trader on the Consumnes River Indian reservation wrote about rapidly gained perspectives on consumerism, "There is not one from the age of ten years up, girl or boy, man or woman, that cannot take their pan, a common milk pan, and go to the river and dig from one dollar to ten in the course of the day, but generally not more than is sufficient for their present wants. If, however, they wish to purchase any article, for instance a horse, they start and in a very few days they can purchase whatever they wish."

A rancher's wife wrote from a five-thousand-acre spread on Stoney Creek, Tehama County, in June 1855, to her sister in Jackson. "Tell henry that my big headed diger has turned out to bee one of the smartes boys in the country. He can wash and cook as well as any person and he can milk eaquel to any woman and he keeps him self neat and clean. We have four of the smartes diger boys in the state of California, which we keep here at the house. Tell henry that we have the rancharee of digers yet and they have worke very faithfull. They cut and bound all of mr. [James M.] Kendrick's grain with reep horse and could have cut four hundred acres at their leasiure."

Today, Native Americans have gained a form of influence and perhaps revenge through legalized gambling. The fifty-seven members of the California Nations Indian Gaming Association operate fifty-four casinos to produce $5 billion a year. As gambling has moved closer to cities, its operators have acquired political clout. Former Governor Gray Davis and Lieutenant Governor Cruz Bustamante benefited hugely from Indian largesse. For instance, San Diego's Viejas Band of Kumeyaay Indians contributed $2 million for Bustamante's campaign during the 2003 recall election.

ANTI-CHINESE SENTIMENT

California's Chinese came from southern China, around Canton. Like everyone else who came to California, they wished to make their fortunes and go home. They moved first into the mines, and then industry. The Chinese, virtually all of whom were single men, settled in their own sections of towns, and looked to the "Six Companies," or benevolent societies, to see to their needs. Factory owners found them good workers for below-average wages, and soon pitted them against American laborers and the emerging workingman's movement. Through piles of books and pamphlets, Californians praised the Chinese far more than any other people of color.

This early welcome gave way to antagonism. In 1852, Governor John Bigler led the charge against Chinese immigration when their numbers reached twenty-five thousand, one-tenth of the population. In some mining counties, Chinese composed one-third of the residents. Although the legislature passed several laws preventing their entry, federal law knocked them all down. In 1859, Shasta County miners began expelling them and other counties did likewise. However, as gold-seekers abandoned exhausted diggings, the Chinese moved in and by 1863 comprised nearly all of the placer miners.

Meanwhile, the battle against the Chinese moved to the cities. In 1859, San Franciscan German cigar makers expelled a member for teaching the trade to Chinese workers; in 1860, ten thousand workingmen petitioned the legislature to bar Asiatics, while their presidential ballots bore the legend, "Anti-Coolie"; in 1861, a San Francisco Anti-Coolie Association emerged; and in 1862, newly inaugurated Republican Governor Leland Stanford supported an immigration ban.

Locally, and singly or in twos and threes, Chinese became part of society. In 1860, one sister in Butte County wrote to another, "I still keep my old Chinaman yet. He is very good help. I have had him near a year." From Auburn, Placer County, that same year, a husband wrote, "We have four boarders and keep a Chinaman that cooks, washes, cuts wood &c. I have to pay him thirty dollars per month."

AFRICAN AMERICANS, SLAVE AND FREE

Though only amounting to less than five thousand Californians in 1860, African Americans established their share of churches, literary societies, private schools, newspapers, and other organizations. Economically, society generally confined them to unskilled labor—they were laborers, miners, cooks, barbers, servants, and waiters. However, Napa County in 1862 had eight African-American farmers, two blacksmiths, two carpenters, three barbers, five wood speculators, five poultry dealers, and four jobbers of merchandise.

"Neither slavery, nor involuntary servitude," said the 1849 state constitution, "shall ever be tolerated in this State." However, California legislators originally from the South refused to enforce this provision, declaring, as an 1852 state supreme court decision said, that it needed "future legislation to carry it out." These politicians kept lengthening the time during which those who had brought slaves into California could use their services. Only in 1858 did the state high court declare this interpretation nonsense.

In 1859, an *Address of the State Executive Committee to the Colored People of the State of California* declared African-American men and women were "Americans by birth and instinct." African Americans were the only disfranchised group to demand civil and political rights. They had to do most of this work alone, as California lacked the organized abolitionist societies of the East. In 1855, 1856, and 1857, angry black conventions met to battle the ban against their testimony in court, and in 1856, they published the San Francisco *Mirror of the Times*.

In 1858, all friends of freedom successfully battled the attempt of a slaveholder to return Archy Lee to a life of servitude in Mississippi, but at the same time, only a parliamentary maneuver by a handful of Republicans kept the legislature from forbidding black immigration to California. In reaction, many families left for Victoria, British Columbia, during the Fraser River Gold Rush. That fall, a demoralized fourth black convention met in San Francisco on October 8, 1858, to consider colonization in Central America and Africa.

SAN FRANCISCO: CALIFORNIA'S CENTER OF CULTURE, FINANCE, MANUFACTURING, AND POPULATION

Much of the history of Gold Rush California is the history of San Francisco. This great port on the Pacific Coast held between a fifth and a fourth of California's population, as men congregated there when unable to mine. It grew from town to city almost instantly, quickly changing from wood to brick. Between December 1849 and June 1851, San Francisco suffered six great fires. Too often, as one formerly prosperous merchant wrote, scorching flames reduced them all to being "beggars in the world." After 1851, the next great fire in the Bay City began on April 18, 1906, after an earthquake.

"Everything rushes along in feverish haste, without rest anywhere," a European observed. However, societal structures did not keep up with the city's physical appearance. Communication with the East by semi-monthly mail steamer took one month in each direction, while importing goods by sailing ship around Cape Horn took from three to six months. Business was chaotic. A Wells Fargo banker remarked in January 1853, "This is the best country that I know of to make money with money," but how could one predict the markets?

A boom and bust cycle became constant, as slow news led easterners to ship goods relying on their best judgment. The results? Overstocked markets, sale by auction of newly arrived cargoes, and the formation of monopolies to bring up prices.

San Francisco was the commercial hub of the Pacific; Montgomery Street was the financial district of San Francisco, and the corner with California Street was its center. In 1865, Grover & Baker's sewing machines and Kennedy & Bell's carpet warehouse end the commercial and residential hotel district. Beyond California Street are two blocks of bankers, assayers, and photographers, overlapping with newspaper publishers and job printers. In 1863, after African Americans gained legal rights, they immediately sued to be allowed to ride the public horse cars.

One merchant astutely observed in June 1854, "There are too many sellers of goods for the amount of population." The climax arrived in February 1855, when California's two largest banks, Page, Bacon & Co. and Adams & Co. failed.

Politicians, of course, intervened. Through the 1850s, no party could really challenge Democratic dominance, so Democrats fought among themselves. The dominant wing comprised "Chivalry" Democrats, from the South, and under aristocratic Senator William M. Gwin, they were firmly committed to slavery and limited constitutional construction. Their consistent challengers were Free-Soilers, who wanted slaves kept out of the nation's common territories, under a pugnacious, self-taught New York workingman, David C. Broderick. His political base included the Irish laborers and fire companies of San Francisco.

The high crime rate had its effect in San Francisco as elsewhere. In 1850 and 1851, it stood at 60 per 100,000, dropping to about 30 for the rest of the decade, and then averaging only 9 per 100,000 in the 1860s. As one Bay City resident remarked in September 1851, "the slow process of law is illy suited to the present population; crime must receive summary punishment."

San Francisco saw two Committees of Vigilance, where merchants set up tribunals to judge and punish criminals. Common crime and destructive fires sweeping through the canvas-and-wood town led to the formation of the first Committee on June 8, 1851. It ultimately had six hundred members, hanged four men, and banished others from the city before disintegrating in September.

Charles Duane was among those banished. A former New York prizefighter, "Dutch Charlie" Duane engaged in much brawling at election time to keep enemies away from the polls. Broderick, himself a veteran of the volunteer fire departments and rough politics of New York City, gathered the toughs that flooded out to California in his never-ending quest for a seat in the U.S. Senate. Duane was one of them. His political friends protected "Dutch Charlie" from the legal consequences of his actions until the 1851 Committee banished him for seven violent brawls, including two attempted murders. However, Duane shortly returned, resuming his interest in politics, the fire department, and fighting.

In March 1855, an opinionated San Francisco wife stated bluntly, "The people are all thieves and cutthroats except me and my husband. We are honest." Certainly, this seemed true of the political world. In 1855, James "Yankee" Sullivan, another prominent prizefighter and "shoulder-striker" (one who punched from the shoulder), who used violence at polling places, elected James P. Casey as a supervisor.

Virtually illiterate, Casey's accounting ability was not the qualification that made him assistant county treasurer for two years. He was not even an announced candidate for election, but a false bottom in a trick ballot box added the needed appropriately marked ballots. Then, a knife fight in August 1855 led a defeated politician to retrieve Casey's New York prison record, which would have murderous consequences the following year.

Two trials in 1856 revealed political bias in homicide and financial cases. First, on November 17, 1855, gambler Charles Cora shot U.S. Marshal William Richardson in personal quarrel over the presence of his mistress, prostitute Belle Cora, among high society. Although the coroner's jury returned a verdict of premeditation, the trial jury in January 1856, due to the famed flowery oratory of attorney Edward D. Baker, failed to reach a verdict.

Another instance of corruption became apparent early in 1856. February 1856 saw a scathing rant from James King of William, the crusading editor of the San Francisco *Bulletin*

57

(who added his father's name after his, in order to set himself apart from all the other "James Kings"). In financial matters, city landowner Broderick favored bankers Palmer, Cook & Co. Heavily involved in politics, this firm had somehow acquired assets and real estate from the collapsed Adams & Co. In February, 1856, Alfred A. Cohen, its receiver of property, came to trial to account for Adams & Co.'s vanished cash and all other assets. Baker was Cohen's attorney. The trial revealed the entire dishonest mess, and although the court held Cohen liable, it never enforced the decision.

The battle between the concerned citizens of San Francisco and corrupt public figures came to a head in May of 1856. On May 14, 1856, the moralistic James King of William denounced Casey as a former convict, "the Sing-Sing man," for all the world to read in the *Bulletin*. Casey promptly shot and killed the editor. The next day, William Tell Coleman revived the Committee of Vigilance. Out of a population of twelve thousand voting men, eight thousand enrolled in the committee. As King went to his grave on May 22, the committee hanged Cora and Casey. Ultimately, it hanged two others and banished many, including brawling Charles Duane. Through August 1856, the Committee of Vigilance defied national, state, and local government.

Why did men join the committee? The corruption of the ballot box was obvious. A real estate broker wrote on May 19, "I for once in my life have given my word of honour under oath to assist and see that the assassin is punished by the people themselves, for our officers in general are a set of gamblers and robbers."

A liquor merchant exclaimed, "Every good and honest man will say, 'God speed the Committee.'" Throughout the summer he reported no sales to his eastern supplier as "all kinds of business has been suspended." For ten years thereafter, the

People's Party, successor to the committee, gave San Francisco good, honest government. Later, Broderick's Democratic Party successors had their day.

PARADISE, AGRICULTURAL AND OTHERWISE

After the hectic 1850s, California settled down in the 1860s. People came to stay. In 1860, the mining counties held one-third of the state's population; in 1870, they only held one-fifth. On December 31, 1860, liquor merchant S.H. Meeker closed out the year by bragging to an eastern friend, "We enjoy the largest liberty, the best climate, and best of every thing that is produced the world over." A well-traveled minister remarked a month later, "California is regarded as a paradise for children." A woman in Knight's Ferry similarly wrote east in March 1861: "Nothing would induce me to return to the states to live."

As time went on, would-be miners turned to other pursuits. Agriculture beckoned most; farmers would supply miners with fresh fruit and vegetables. One farmer's wife wrote in October 1854, "The Sacramento Valley is the richest land in the world and a farm here is a fortune." Her husband, who had been setting out fruit trees, added, "This is the short way to make money here now."

Another Californian wrote from San Andreas in March 1858, uncertain as to his employment: "I am at 3 & 4 kinds of business. First is I am a ranching and then I am in the Nurserry business. Then I have to peddle my trees & then I have a mining claime that I have worked; then I am ingauged in the Murreys Creek union ditch. Today I was a planting potatoes & So you can see that it is one thing and then another."

By 1860, California exported wheat, rather than being an importer, and soon it dominated the world market. California

59

Four horses push a McCormick header through a Central Valley field, dumping the grain into the low side of the wagon that moved along with it, while a farm worker constantly leveled the load. From the 1860s through the 1880s, California was the unsurpassed breadbasket of the world.

flour meant quality. Count Agoston Haraszthy of Hungary popularized California winemaking through learned writings. Haraszthy also imported two hundred thousand wine cuttings from Europe to improve California grape stock. His 1858 Buena Vista winery near Sonoma still produces.

At the same time, as mining strikes burst upon Nevada, the rest of the American West, and around the world, some forty San Francisco foundries supplied mining and milling machines. Innovations ranged from huge engines to raise and lower miners and ore, Cornish pumps to keep the mines dry, pounding batteries of stamps to crush ore, and separators and amalgamators to recover the gold. By 1870, the Golden State ranged twenty-fourth in population among thirty-seven states and sixteenth in manufacturing output. San Francisco stock exchanges emerged to supply capital to burgeoning Nevada mines. The vast majority of mine promoters never found gold or silver, but mined stock purchasers through assessments; they required additional sums of money to allegedly carry on mining operations.

Culture Comes to the Far West

California attracted people with talent and initiative. They needed courage to move to a faraway land. The state's bounty promoted exaggeration in everything from huge fruits, vegetables, and trees, to splendid mountains, abundant game, and a temperate climate. Perhaps to fit their surroundings, all the settlers seemed to have titles, such as "Colonel," "General," "Judge," and so on. Recognizing that somehow Californians were special, those who had arrived before January 1, 1850, formed the Society of California Pioneers on August 31 of that year, setting themselves apart from all later arrivals.

By 1860, when California stood only twenty-fourth in population among thirty-four states, the Golden State ranked eleventh in the number of newspapers. The Bay City had forty-five, representing almost every local interest, and in the interior of the state there were eighty. Edward C. Kemble even wrote a book-length history of the press, which appeared in the Christmas 1858 issue of the Sacramento *Union*, the paper of record for the state.

In spite of being in such an "instant state," the arts flourished. Literary weeklies and monthlies, such as the *Pioneer, Golden Era, Hutchings' California Magazine*, and the 1868 *Overland*

Monthly carried the words of authors still read today. Writers of the 1850s and 1860s included Ina Coolbrith, the state's first poet laureate, Dame Shirley (Louise Clappe), Adah Isaacs Menken, Ambrose (Bitter) Bierce, J. Ross Browne, humorist George Horatio Derby, known as John Squibob or Phoenix; Alonzo Delano (Old Block), Bret Harte, the Reverend Thomas Starr King, Joaquin Miller, John Rollin Ridge (Yellow Bird), William H. "Caxton" Rhodes, an early science fiction writer; poet Edward Rowland Sill, Charles Warren Stoddard, and Mark Twain (Samuel L. Clemens). Strangely, by 1870, most of these writers were gone.

Culture and the life of the mind advanced as Californians came to settle. Education improved on many fronts. Often, religious leaders furthered schooling. In March 1850, San Francisco made Baptist John C. Pelton's free school the first public school in California. San Jose Methodists incorporated what is now Stockton's University of the Pacific on July 10, 1851. The year 1853 saw the Congregational Reverends Henry Durant and Samuel H. Willey inaugurate the College of California in Oakland, which in 1868 became the University of California. In 1855, Jesuits founded the University of San Francisco, while in 1863, Archbishop Joseph Sadoc Alemany started Moraga's St. Mary's College.

To aid the self-educated, who studied in snatches, libraries came to the fore. Private, fee-charging ones came before today's standard public libraries. The Monterey Library Association appeared in 1849. In San Francisco, the Mercantile Library Association opened in 1853, and the Independent Order of Odd Fellows' Library Association emerged in 1855. The Mechanics' Institute Library, similarly funded by member subscriptions beginning in 1854, still flourishes at 57 Post Street. The Institute sponsored near-annual fairs between 1857 and 1899 showcasing California manufacturers. The California

State Library, now in Sacramento, opened in January 1850, and enlarging its original function for use by government officers, its research collections are priceless today.

Fine art and photography were among Mechanics' Fair exhibits in the 1850s and 1860s. Viewers admired mining and California scenes by such notables as Charles Nahl, Thomas A. Ayers, and William S. Jewett. Cartoonist Edward Jump was just one of many talented Frenchmen that Californians could view in commercial galleries.

The wonders of the Golden State thrilled photographers within a decade of that technology's invention. Noted ones included George R. Fardon, whose bound panoramic shots of San Francisco in 1856 became the first public viewbook of any American city. A decade later, Carleton Watkins artistically showed the world the glories of the Yosemite Valley.

Californians, from city dwellers to inhabitants of remote mining camps, went to the theater, and during the 1850s they saw over one thousand different plays. Traveling companies roamed the mining camps. Shakespeare remained the favorite. Popular acts included Lola Montez, performer of the notorious "spider dance," who discovered child star Lotta Crabtree at age eight; Adah Isaacs Menken, a sexy actress as well as a poet; and theater stalwarts Junius and Edwin Booth and Edwin Forrest.

Above all, Californians remained curious. In 1853, the San Francisco Academy of Natural Sciences, now the oldest in the West, came into being. Its founders planned "a thorough systematic survey of every portion of the State and the collection of a cabinet of her rare and rich productions." By 1857, "already the Academy is in possession of specimens so numerous and varied, as to render a visit to its rooms one of peculiar interest and pleasure," one who accepted their invitation declared. Editor James Mason Hutchings, who shortly became the foremost promoter of Yosemite Valley, marveled of "a magnificent specimen" of a seven-foot yucca tree brought up from San Diego. Today, the Academy holds 18 million such natural treasures. *Hutchings' California Magazine*, stuffed with fine woodblocks and descriptive articles, began in July 1856 "to picture California, and California life" to the world.

SECTIONAL STRIFE ENGULFS CALIFORNIA

David C. Broderick finally became a U.S. Senator in 1857, but the prize merely brought him disappointment and death. The feud that would be his downfall openly erupted in 1859 as a precursor to the Civil War. President James Buchanan, a weak Southern sympathizer, denied Broderick any patronage, forcing Broderick to organize a separate Free-Soiler Democratic Party organization.

At the Democratic Party convention that summer, David S. Terry, a Texan and chief justice of the California Supreme Court, declared Broderick's party to be no longer Democrats and a group of "Negro Lovers" besides. The result was a duel between Broderick and Terry following the Democratic sweep of the election, and Broderick fell mortally wounded at the first fire. His death on September 16, 1859, began a political revolution that led to Republican victory in the 1860 presidential election and in the race for governor in 1861.

The Civil War of 1861 indeed turned the political tables in California. The Southern philosophy and actions of mainstream Democrats branded the formerly powerful majority "traitors." If "Constitutional guarantees" could not preserve the Union, the state Democratic Party declared in 1861 and 1862 when fighting was heavy, then "we are in favor of the recognition of the independence of the Confederate States."

The notably eccentric James Lick arrived in San Francisco in January 1848, invested wisely in real estate, and, indicative of California scientific inquisitiveness, left a fortune to build the most powerful telescope in the world. His choice of Mount Hamilton near San Jose brought into existence the first permanently occupied mountain observatory. In 1888 the Great Refractor Telescope—today the second largest of its type—first peered at the heavens. Run by the University of California, Lick Observatory is in the forefront of astronomical discoveries.

Minority status and Unionist contempt followed. California's eight regiments of infantry, two of cavalry, and other smaller units fought Indians, guarded the central and southern overland mail routes, and watched local secessionists.

Though it had a border state population of Northerners and Southerners, California became firmly on the side of the Union. Perhaps distance from the rest of the battling states made California's heart grow fonder of the Union. Some Golden State laws against enemy supporters were earlier and harsher than those of eastern states. Voters continually elected Unionists to office, silenced Southerners, doubled the number of militia companies to 123 in 1864, and contributed one quarter of the $5 million that the United States Sanitary Commission, a forerunner in function of the Red Cross, raised nationally.

Southerners quietly went back east to fight, and within California, they collected money to aid "Rebs" in Northern prison camps. On March 15, 1863, three conspirators attempted to convert the *J.M. Chapman*, a small schooner, into a Confederate commerce raider to attack the gold-carrying mail steamers. Their immediate apprehension provoked the legislature to pass a raft of legislation banning treasonable practices and making California the first state to inaugurate loyalty oaths for attorneys, schoolteachers, swamp land purchasers, and harbor pilots.

A few rural newspapers became obstreperous. In November 1862, Long Primer Hall, a huge jovial Mississippian of the Visalia *Equal Rights Expositor* rewrote Governor Leland Stanford's Thanksgiving Prayer: "O, Lord, we thank thee for letting the rebels wallop us at the battle of Pittsburg Landing [Shiloh]—for letting them smite us hip and thigh, even unto the destruction of 96,000 of our good 'loyal' soldiers, and 463 of our officers, and for giving speed to their legs through the awful swamps of the Chickahominy. . . ."

On March 15, 1863, the government seized the schooner J.M. Chapman,
*which Confederates planned to use to despoil the Pacific Mail Steamers
of their golden cargo. An outraged legislature reacted by requiring the
first loyalty oaths in the nation, strengthened the national guard, generally increased security, and provided a precedent for a 1949 Red Scare
loyalty oath. (*Pictorial War Record, *1865.)*

The next year, Rowena Granice Steele, the editor of the Snelling *Merced Banner*, named her son Jefferson Davis Lee Stonewall Jackson Richmond Steele. The government half-heartedly banned a half-dozen such papers from the mails to cut their circulation, with little effect, and on three occasions, companies of California Volunteers tossed their type (individual lead letters) into the street. The newspapers penned by Hall and Steele were two of the targets.

As during the Gold Rush, Californians spurned Federal monetary policy. With mountains of gold, California repudiated government-issued paper money, the value of which depended on the war news. In July 1863, after the Union victories at Gettysburg and Vicksburg, greenbacks stood at 76 cents on the gold dollar. In July 1864, with General Ulysses S. Grant stalled before Richmond and General William Tecumseh Sherman stopped in front of Atlanta, currency hit a low of 38 cents. When the chief Treasury official of the Pacific Coast tried to promote currency at a gold meeting in February 1864, the crowd chased him from the building with shouts of "Hang him! Hang him!"

Civil Rights Revolution

Though California escaped armed strife during the Civil War period, the battle of ideas was ever present. In 1860, Republican orator Edward D. Baker proclaimed, "Democracy in the United States means equal rights to *all sections*"—hence protection for Southern slavery, "and Republicanism means equal rights to all men." These two opposing philosophies were on a collision course, and each had to destroy the other's most cherished principles to survive.

With Republican ascendancy, the African American community revived. First, a vigorous press emerged, when Peter Anderson and Philip A. Bell brought out the *Pacific Appeal* on March 29, 1862, followed by the *Elevator* under Bell, on March 31, 1865, to appeal for civil rights and elevate African Americans. By 1862, supporters of a united nation, regardless of previous political party, fused as the Union Party, and black men and women received basic rights.

On the national scene, President Abraham Lincoln provisionally on September 22, 1862, and permanently on January 1, 1863, freed all Southern slaves. "The Year of Jubilee Has Come!" shouted the black press. Due to constitutional restraints on his authority, Lincoln authorized emancipation under his war powers. This excluded all recaptured areas then under Union army control. The U.S. Constitution governed this former Southern territory and exempted it from proclamation provisions.

The freeing of Southern slaves emboldened California Unionists and forged factional Democrats into one party opposed to the war and emancipation. "Every privilege conferred upon a fugitive black," one paper charged, "represents a right or privilege wrested from a persecuted white." The Thirteenth Amendment to the Constitution, ratified in 1865 at the close of the war, officially ended slavery and removed the last legal quibbles.

In California, the basic, fundamental right of testimony in all court cases, civil and criminal, was granted to African Americans during the 1863 session of the legislature. San Franciscans promptly used this right to sue successfully, after several years' battle, to ride the horse-drawn street railroad cars. Next, in 1864 Bay City blacks gained a separate public school, and beginning in 1865, grudgingly had permission to participate in Independence Day celebrations with everyone else.

The fifth and final African American convention held in Sacramento on October 25, 1865, battled for broader public education throughout California and through the 1870s fought through the court system to bring integrated schools.

On the Federal level, the General Land Office in Washington in 1862 ruled on a Marysville case that African Americans could indeed legally settle and acquire public land. Furthermore, black men could serve as soldiers and sailors. Many returned east to fight, some served in auxiliary positions with the California Volunteers, and in 1864, Maryland freedmen, in groups of twenty-five, served on the ships of the Pacific Squadron.

By the 1864 presidential election, Unionists had full political control of the state. On July 21, 1864, Charles L. Weller, Chairman of the Democratic State Central Committee, the highest-ranking party official, declared that the military would prevent Democrats from voting. "I counsel Brute Force," he yelled, as he called on party members to "arm," and form secret societies "now," to "resist the high arm of military tyranny in California."

Unfortunately for Weller, he made these irrational remarks where Union Leaguers could hear them. The secret Union League, almost a quasi-government in itself, had most federal, state, and local leaders as members among 140 statewide councils, which often allied with militia companies. The League secretary promptly sent a transcript of the speech to General Irvin McDowell, commanding the military Department of the Pacific.

Weller soon had quarters on cold, grim Fort Alcatraz, while the commanding general wondered, "Whether the public safety will admit of Mr. Weller's release to join his friends, or will require his friends shall be sent to join him." Unionists told Democratic foes, "We insist that Weller be read out of the party, or that party assumes the responsibility of his offense."

Fort Point, completed in 1861 and now a popular tourist destination underneath the picturesque Golden Gate Bridge (1937), is architecturally similar to Fort Sumter in Charleston Harbor. It joined with Fort Alcatraz to defend San Francisco. Two boys watch the Matson liner Mariposa *(1931) sail past.*

In the last grand Democratic rally before the vote between Abraham Lincoln and General George B. McClellan, headlines from the San Francisco *Democratic Press* and the *American Flag* graphically illustrated contrasting polemical viewpoints and illuminated the nature of journalism at the time.

First, the Democratic Party version of this parade:

> "The Last Grand Charge of the McClellan Men of San Francisco—The Queen City of the Pacific in a Blaze of Democratic Glory—Abe Lincoln is Wanted in Illinois, the People Want Little Mac in Washington—Let the Cannon Peal, the Bells Ring and the People Shout for Joy, for the Reign of Blood and Slaughter is Drawing to its Close."

A foaming radical wing of the Union party saw this event differently:

> "The Last Grand Scramble of the Gorillas!—Howls, Roars, Groans, Yelps, Yells, Red Fire, Rages, and Blue Blazes!—The [Irish] Species on Horseback, on Foot, in Buggies, in Hacks, on Drays, in Swill Carts and Mud Boxes!—Broom Rangers, Steamship Rioters, Aliens and Reprobates Howl Themselves Hoarse!—Death on a Pale Horse, and All Hell Following Him!"

The culmination of wartime hysteria came on April 15, 1865, a bright California day that quickly turned to gloom and darkness when the telegraph flashed the news of the assassination of President Abraham Lincoln. "The people fairly staggered under the blow," one woman declared, "There was wildness and madness and the most intense excitement in every eye." San Francisco witnessed the strongest tension, as the first mob in the city's history destroyed property, including many newspapers due to their opposition to the Lincoln Administration—one Democratic, two Irish-Catholic, one British, and two French. That night, bonfires blazed in downtown intersections as troops patrolled the streets.

With local authorities fearful to act, General Irvin McDowell, commanding the military department, ordered the arrest of all "so utterly infamous as to exult over the assassination of the President." Between April 17 and June 1, 1865, the Army arrested sixty-eight California traitors. The largest number excavated for the brick Casemated Barracks on Fort Alcatraz, where tour boats now dock, and some sang about their problems:

> What a sad sight to see six and thirty men once free,
> Imprisoned for expressing an opinion!
> And when this noble band are made to shovel sand
> There's cursing in the happy land of Canaan!

On January 13, 1865, San Franciscans were the first in the nation to name a school after Abraham Lincoln. On April 14, 1866, they dedicated the first statue to the martyred president.

With the war ending, California entered the Reconstruction era, when the Southern states would be remade. The nation reflected a strong push for civil rights. On January 5, 1865, the San Jose *Mercury* was "In the Van" as the first California paper to advocate black suffrage, just as it had been in October 1861 the first paper to call for emancipation. A week later, editor James Jerome Owen was the first to advocate women's suffrage.

The African American Sacramento convention convened in late 1865 "to obtain the highest privilege of Citizenship, the Elective Franchise." Voting for black men came in 1870, though not from state action, but rather through national ratification of the Fifteenth Amendment to the federal Constitution.

While Unionists worked for rights for disfranchised African Americans, they wished to curtail voting privileges of other non-citizens. They cut into the foreign-born foundation of Democratic Party support through an 1866 voter registration law to block "the most base-faced frauds." Too many immigrants, according to Unionists, voted Democratic without becoming legal citizens.

Military victory in 1865 rearranged California political parties again. With the Union preserved, those who refused to grant civil and political rights to black men and the Chinese joined a revived Democratic party. In 1867, a San Francisco street contractor employed thirty Chinese for work traditionally done by the Irish. On February 12, four hundred Irish workers attacked, killing one Chinese and burning two boardinghouses.

Eight days later, Irish workingmen, Democratic political supporters, and the Eight Hour (workday) Men from twenty-two trade unions joined to form the Anti-Coolie Association. They united to combat the "fearful influx of Asiatic serfs." The threat of Sunday Laws then brought German voters into the Democratic ranks. Democrats captured governorship and state offices in 1867 and the legislature and Supreme Court in 1869. Their legislature promptly "disapproved and rejected" the Fifteenth Amendment.

Through the late 1860s, declining Republican legislative power fought to grant court testimony to Chinese. Before the war, mining counties and urban workingmen opposed rights for the Chinese; now the cleavage came on straight political lines. A comprehensive revision of all California laws, which went into effect in January 1873, removed the last barriers to Chinese and Indian testimony.

THE RAILROAD!

The war also brought an "Iron Horse" from the East. The Pacific Railroad symbolized Californians' hopes and dreams from the first days of the new state. Californians demanded a transcontinental railroad, but congressional and sectional battles would delay its inauguration for years. The strict interpretation of federal powers under the Constitution by Southern legislators would not allow government sponsorship.

First came an overland stagecoach mail route. After years of the usual squabbles and delay, in 1857, Congress authorized a dusty, twenty-eight-hundred-mile, semi-weekly mail route from St. Louis, Missouri, to San Francisco, by way of El Paso, Texas, and Los Angeles. To get the mail contract, Vice President John Butterfield of the American Express Co. brought in directors from the three other mighty express companies in the nation, Adams Express Co., United States Express Co., and California's Wells, Fargo & Co., to form the Overland Mail Company.

Stagecoach mail service began in September 1858, and mail arrived so promptly within the twenty-five-day contract time that by spring 1860, stagecoaches carried more letters than the semi-monthly mail steamers. In March 1861, the coming Civil War shifted the mail line north, running through Salt Lake City.

Where national and sectional influences left off, local rivalries grew to check railroad building. In February 1856, engineer Theodore D. Judah finished the Sacramento Valley Railroad, which ran twenty-two miles to Folsom. While that line replaced Sacramento as the stagecoach hub for the mines, the bankrupt railroad went into receivership to French bankers in San Francisco. In the 1860s, these financiers joined Bay City Democrats and Wells, Fargo & Co., to build a railroad

A six-horse stagecoach bound for Oregon passes soaring Mount Shasta. This was public transportation, 1871, a bit (12.5 cents) a mile and all the dust you could eat. Speed was five miles an hour for all twenty-four of the day. (Courtesy of Wells Fargo.)

over the Sierra on the bustling, jammed wagon road through Placerville to the Comstock. Greed and incompetence stalled their efforts.

When the Sacramento Valley Railroad dumped Judah in 1860 for publicly suggesting a route through Auburn, he turned to other supporters. The great railroad stood as a solid plank in the Republican Party platform. On June 28, 1861, four Sacramento hardware and dry goods merchants, who were founders of the California's 1856 Republican Party, agreed to support Judah's dreams and formed the Central Pacific Railroad Company. Together, they completed the project, in spite of continued opposition from San Francisco political and financial interests, bad weather, bad luck, and the background of the Civil War. These Big Four were Leland Stanford, governor of California and the company's politician; Collis P. Huntington, a master of the Washington lobby; Mark Hopkins, money man; and Charles Crocker, construction supervisor.

On July 1, 1862, Congress passed the Pacific Railroad bill naming the Central Pacific Company as the western builder, and on January 8, 1863, as a large mural in the Sacramento Amtrak station shows, they broke ground. Yet few purchased railroad stocks and bonds, making funding a continual concern. Scrounging credit wherever they could, the four principals paid as they could to keep construction going. Workers laid the first rail on October 23, 1863, and on April 26, 1864, trains ran to Roseville. These fifty miles cost $2.25 million.

Early in 1865, Charles Crocker began an experiment. His brother, Judge Edwin Bryant Crocker wrote on April 12, "A large part of our force are Chinese and they prove nearly equal to white men in the amount of labor they perform, and are far more reliable. We are training them to all kinds of labor, blasting, driving horses, handling rock, as well as the pick and shovel." The track reached Colfax, fifty-four miles from Sacramento, on

September 1, 1865, and parties began working on the tunnels. "On the road we are having a hell of a time just now," a worker stated on November 19. "This week it has rained nearly all the time and there is mud without bottom."

The railroad chuffed into Cisco in December 1866, having cost $8.5 million through that summer. Tunneling continued through 1867, and engineers developed thirty-seven miles of snowsheds protecting the track in 1868 (and, to protect forests, in 1870 they added fire-fighting trains). Ten thousand workers, mostly Chinese, pushed steadily forward. Through trains arrived in Reno on June 18, 1868, and then entered a race with the westward-building Union Pacific Railroad to fix each road's territory. On May 10, 1869, a gold spike joined the transcontinental railroad at Promontory, Utah. One toast to Crocker and his workers summed up their accomplishment: "The Pacific Railroad—the only piece of Crocker-y ware made out of China."

After twenty years of immigration and settlement, what did it mean to be a Californian? What was the interaction between risk-taking, natural bounty, luck, and the special quality of California? Hannah A. Rines thought she knew. Since Californians were in too much of a hurry to take the time to cook, she found a niche. Rines wrote to her brother in Maine, from the town of Washington, Yolo County, across the river from Sacramento on December 1, 1860:

"We arieved hear the 12 of Aprail [1860] and Richard went to haying the next week and has had employment ever since. We are shure to get enough to eat for I do the cooking for choice. There are very poor cooks in this place. California is noted for that. I have 25 dollars per month work. Eight months I have only spent thirty five of that, for I want the interest. It is a cent an a ½ on a dollar a month."

Painter and railroad photographer Alfred A. Hart captured a shiny 1860s Central Pacific engine charging ahead through the Lost Camp Spur Cut, eighty miles from Sacramento. Where others failed, a talented, persevering group of four major investors realized their vision of a transcontinental railroad.

At the end of the decade, her family fortunes had changed dramatically. Now she wrote from the Yolo County seat of Woodland on October 26, 1869:

> "Our Bills ar all paid and prepaid to put in a nother crop. We have upward of fifty tones of grain in the sacks all ready for market. I have sold 286.40 dollars worth of Butter [in] just one year and eggs $179.31, and I have a great many chickens to sell. We have seven large hogs to kill; fatted them on apples.
>
> "We have 10 horses, two Wagons, 1 Buggy, all Kinds of farming tools, House Hold furniture. We Bought four carpets last Aprail; paid 60 dollars for them in smoak meat. I paid 30 dollars for feathers to make me a nice bead. I have a nice stuft Chair, 2 rocking chairs, 6 cain seated chairs, 1 stand, 1 center table, two large dishes enough to set down a harvest crew a bout 20 men and other things. Accordly a plenty of fruit. We have money and dets all paid. That is the best of all Excepting health."

Arriving with nothing, in ten years Hannah Rines had succeeded. She found the California dream!

CHAPTER III

Be Careful What You Wish For: The Railroad Years
(1870–1900)

Californians got their railroad. Immediately, cheap goods flooded in from the East, inhibiting manufacturing, increasing layoffs, and intensifying the conflict with Chinese labor. Soon the Central/Southern Pacific Railroad controlled river and coastal transportation, crushed independent newspapers, and bought the state legislature. At the same time, though, the hated "Octopus" also opened up agricultural land for settlement, sponsored scientific studies of soils and crops, and led the fight for national parks. A political cartoon in the early 1880s popularized the image of the railroad as a grasping, multi-armed animal.

California also came of age during the final years of the nineteenth century. Outsiders began to remark on the uniqueness of the Golden State. It really was something special. Its distinctiveness impressed political scholar James Bryce of England, who came in 1881 and 1883. He declared in his definitive two-volume study of federal, state, and local government, *The American Commonwealth* (1888), that, after traveling the nation widely, the state of California was "in many respects the most striking in the whole Union." Bryce viewed such great

In 1889, horse cars and cable cars crowd the entrance to the Central Pacific Railroad's Oakland, Alameda, and Berkeley Ferry Building. Sidewheel ferries connected San Franciscans to trains running east from the Mole near today's Treasure Island. The signs above the entrance bays reveal the great reach of the "Octopus" railroad: Napa, Calistoga, Yuma (Arizona), Portland (Oregon), Chicago (Illinois), and New York.

diversity in geography, climate, population, and economy to expound that California had "the character of a great country, capable of standing alone in the world."

With vast revenues flowing in, the railroad became the dominant power. World-renowned reformer Henry George, then a struggling journalist, raised pertinent questions early. In the fourth issue of *The Overland Monthly* he asked in October 1868, "What Will the Railroad Bring Us?" On the income side of the ledger, George noted, "It will be the means of converting a wilderness into a populous empire."

At about 1907, passengers at Los Angeles use fast, inexpensive rail travel to head toward Salt Lake City. Black porters help well-dressed women board an ornate Pullman car. Such service jobs became reserved for African Americans. In the 1920s, the sleeping car porters' union led the drive for higher salaries and better working conditions. (Photograph by Warren C. Dickerson.)

COME TO CALIFORNIA!

How do you transform "a wilderness into a populous empire?" Bring in productive people. Beginning with the legislatively funded California Immigrant Union in 1870 and running through the 1930s, graphically beautiful literature called immigrants to the land of perpetual summer. "This is a land of Sunshine," a new arrival enthused in 1887, "and of flowers almost too pretty for the eye to look on." In fact, he wrote from San Jose, "Every thing that is put in the ground and watered will

83

Luther and Eliza Tibbets of Riverside started a southern California industry in 1875 with the winter-ripening Washington Naval Orange. A year later, San Gabriel's A.B. Chapman began growing Valencias, which came to market at other times of the year. In the early twentieth century, year-round oranges became an icon of California's endless summer.

grow and produce largely." People came, generally to Northern California and the Central Valley, but with the land "Boom of the 1880s" into Southern California as well. The railroad brought out New York journalist Charles Nordhoff, who captured the allure in *California for Health, Pleasure, and Residence* (1872).

A wife in Delano wrote to her parents in the centennial year, 1876: "I think if you spent one winter in California you would never want to spend another in Maine. You would only be seven or eight days on the road and every thing is nice as it can be on the cars. You could take a sleeping car all the way through." Ten years later, an observer from the same area remarked, "The railroads are doing a big business now, I can tell you. There are thousands of people coming into this state every month. It is going to be the making of this state, as most of them will settle down here, and buy land."

Here is a glimpse of life in Los Angeles before the railroad came. A settler wrote to his brother on July 3, 1882, "We live now 1½ miles from the Post Office and 50 rods [250 meters] from the Horse Cars, 'fare 5 cents.' The House is one story, three rooms, and ¼ acre land, fenced, is set out with Fruit trees all bearing well—apples, pears, peaches, grapes, persimmons, nectarines, pomegranates. We have water in the yard from the Water Works. The rent is $5 for the House and $2 for water a month."

The influx of new arrivals via the railroad sparked a Southern California land boom. In 1885, $185 brought immigrants from the wintry Midwest to enjoy the warm, healthy California climate. However, as the Southern Pacific Railroad built east and the Santa Fe came west, fares plummeted. On March 7, 1887, the railroads cut rates to $1, but in practice fares settled at $25 or less.

That summer, promoters sold any land they could get their hands on, and $100 million worth of real estate changed hands. One sister wrote to another on May 29, 1887, from National City, San Diego County, "Real estate is *going up,* a flying." In that decade, Los Angeles grew from eleven thousand to eighty thousand people, and the region gained one hundred and thirty thousand permanent settlers—large numbers then, although minuscule today.

At the end of the old century and on the cusp of the new, the solitude of the land, as well as the purity and simplicity of the native cultures of Southern California—both Californio and Native American—and the Southwest exerted a calming

85

influence. Booster Charles Fletcher Loomis said it all with the title of his 1895 magazine, *Land of Sunshine*. Pasadena exemplified warmth in 1890, holding the first Tournament of Roses Parade on New Year's Day, when winter was everywhere else. The year 1902 brought Rose Bowl football.

Vast spaces bearing the marks of Spanish and Indian heritage infused everything from the clean lines of Mission Revival furniture (popularized by Gustav Stickley), adobe and tile Mission Revival architecture, and George Wharton James' still-useful studies of Native American crafts, through Robinson Jeffers' early poems and Maynard Dixon's paintings. Like many, Mary Austin found the land healing and inspirational as she wrote about life in the Owens Valley in *The Land of Little Rain* (1903).

WRITING BOOKS AND READING THEM

The rest of California also saw the flowering of a unique regional culture. In 1854, when Boston funded its Free Public Library through taxation, it started a nationwide movement. Two decades later, in 1878, state Senator George H. Rogers of San Francisco provided public funds for the founding of local libraries. Los Angeles became the first city in California to seize this opportunity. Oakland's public library also began that that year, with poet laureate and contemporary literary luminary Ina D. Coolbrith as librarian. Sacramento and San Francisco followed in 1879, and San Jose and Stockton did so in 1880. In the Bay City, diverse leaders including Andrew Hallidie, Henry George, and Dennis Kearny, led the drive to gather books.

Between 1899 and 1921, steel baron Andrew Carnegie funded 142 free public libraries in California; the first were in

San Diego, Oakland, and Alameda. All were urban—except for one. In 1915, the farmers around Bayliss, Glenn County, which did not even have a post office, were determined to have a library. These knowledge-hungry residents roughly in the middle of nowhere badgered the Carnegie Foundation, and Bayliss Library opened on July 14, 1917. Although the smallest of all two thousand built, Bayliss Library has operated continually and in 2001 justly became marked as a California Point of Historic Interest.

Hubert Howe Bancroft did his best to fill those libraries. He began as a bookseller, and by the end of his life he realized a dream—a "history factory." The indefatigable Bancroft collected all he could: family papers, commercial broadsides, ephemeral pamphlets, throwaway newspapers, and nearly sixty thousand books. To gain unwritten knowledge, he ambitiously commissioned oral histories. H.H. Bancroft did not remain a mere collector of knowledge. With numerous writing assistants, he put the material to work. Within forty years of the start of the American period in California, Bancroft (and his writers) had written the history of the West, from Alaska to Central America, and from the Pacific Coast to all the states in line with Colorado. His thirty-nine volumes have neither been equaled nor supplanted.

Years before Bancroft's history of the West, California's gold-seekers knew they were special. Besides the 1850 Society of California Pioneers, the California Historical Society emerged in 1871, and carpenter Albert M. Winn formed another society in 1875. He had been a forty-niner, a leading city councilman and the father of Sacramento's city government that year, and in 1867 he championed the eight-hour workday. Now he founded the Native Sons of the Golden West, preparing the new generation to preserve the history and historic sites of his adopted state. It still carries out his legacy.

Adolph Sutro, who became mayor of San Francisco in 1894, also promoted the collection of knowledge for the public good. Beginning in 1882, he collected a two hundred-and-fifty-thousand-volume public research library. His would be "a library of reference" for the "benefit of the people among whom I have so long labored." It became the largest private library in the nation at a time when the University of California Library held only eighty thousand books. Sutro specialized in scientific and technical works, but he also collected superb holdings in colonial and revolutionary Mexico, seventeenth-century England, ancient Jewish manuscripts, and one-seventh of the then-known copies of fifteenth-century printed books. Unfortunately, the fire of 1906 halved its holdings, while lack of an endowment hindered the library's maintenance and development. Now owned by the state of California, the Sutro Library is housed at San Francisco State University and specializes in genealogy.

Individual books also became important. In this baroque Gilded Age of robust capitalism and garish conspicuous consumption, reform did not disappear. Writer Helen Hunt Jackson looked to Native Americans, just as her friend Harriet Beecher Stowe had dramatized the plight of slaves in *Uncle Tom's Cabin* (1852). When the country ignored Jackson's serious study, *A Century of Dishonor* (1881), she, too, wrote a novel. The still-popular *Ramona* (1884) dramatizes the sufferings of former Southern California mission Indians, who, ignored and cheated, were barely surviving.

In the general field of fine arts, writers Henry George and Robert Louis Stevenson made names for themselves, while Isadora Duncan, offspring of an innovative journalistic and literary clan, blended motion and form to create modern dance. The San Francisco Art Association in 1871 drew together the region's greatest landscape painters—Albert Bierstadt, Andrew

Adolph Sutro's second Cliff House (1896–1907), the most fanciful of three, exudes turn-of-the-century confidence as it juts out over the ocean by San Francisco. The middle class enjoyed leisure time at the beach—but no bikinis here!

P. Hill, and William Keith, among others, while Jules Tavernier became the best-known French painter. Photographer Eadweard Muybridge became famous worldwide for his San Francisco city panoramas done in 1877 and 1878, and for his studies in motion. Movies still run at twenty-four frames per second, the standard Muybridge set for a series of still photographs capturing the motion of a running horse.

GROSS INEQUALITIES IN WEALTH

However, in 1868, George saw more entries on the railroad's debit side. He feared the "concentration of wealth." George reasoned, "The more dense population and more thorough development of the wealth of the State," he wrote, "will be to a reduction both of the rate of interest and the rate of wages." Therefore, "Those who have, it will make wealthier; for those who have not, it will make it more difficult to get."

George was correct. In the 1870s, wealth built on the transcontinental railroad, on Comstock silver, and on monopolized commerce rebuilt San Francisco. Andrew Hallidie, a maker of wire ropes for suspension bridges and mining machinery, turned his creative genius in 1873 to the invention of the cable car. Now, with cheap public transportation that climbed San Francisco's highest hills, magnates' mansions began to appear, most notably up California Street on the top of Nob Hill. George saw this concentration of wealth, declared land to be the basis of all wealth—unlike Karl Marx, who gave that honor to labor—and developed the nationally known "Single Tax" theory. Land monopolists, of course, would pay the most under his plan.

California's capitalists had little to fear with California Democrat Stephen J. Field on the U.S. Supreme Court. This

Andrew Hallidie's 1873 invention of the cable car saved horses and allowed San Francisco's elite to build atop Nob Hill. Although the state-supported silk industry failed, in 1883, Edward Carlson & James P. Currier displayed the mechanics of the new transportation. The railroad brought its builders millions, as lavishly exhibited in the opulent homes, between Powell and Mason Streets, of President Leland Stanford and Treasurer Mark Hopkins.

In 1892, an owner and master builder pose in back of a nearly completed mansion in the Castro district of San Francisco. The real stars, though, are the twenty carpenters standing tall up to the lightning rod. Now divided into rental apartments, the building still stands at the intersection of Douglass and Caselli.

ambitious justice, who holds the record for court longevity, held sacred the rights of property. Huge landed estates grew. Speculators, such as butchers and cattlemen Henry Miller and Charles Lux, as well as cotton planter James Ben Ali Haggin and his brother-in-law Lloyd Tevis, were able to accumulate millions of acres. Cheaply, they purchased alternate railroad land grant townships and tapped government largesse in swamps and arid lands. These largely worthless acres, though, bloomed with irrigation and therefore became valuable. Their epic battles over water developed irrigation techniques and brought court-settled riparian law.

In 1887, Democratic Assemblyman C.C. Wright of Stanislaus introduced a law that allowed farmer-formed irrigation districts (Haggin's position) to take precedent over the unrestricted water use from English common law for those who lived along the rivers (Miller and Lux's argument).

While millionaires lived in luxury, strife became rampant in the San Francisco workingmen's "tar flats" below Nob Hill and south of Market Street, and throughout the Golden State. As George predicted, prices and wages fell because cheaper goods poured in from Chicago and manufacturing centers further east.

"The Pacific Rail Road does not seem to have helped us here at all," a Tehama rancher complained in October 1869. "On the contrary, times are harder here now than ever." In June 1870, a San Francisco merchant remarked, "Times are dull every where. We are not selling half of the amount of lumber out of the yard that we were last year at this time, and to look ahead, the prospects are nothing."

An observer closed the year 1887 perceptively pointing to "the one great draw back" of the Golden State: "No manufacturing of any consequence." California could not compete with the East. With few such jobs, "the poorer classes have to shift about in order to live."

California production shone only in areas where it had rich natural resources or advantages. Iron foundries, such as the 1849 Union Iron Works, supplied mining machinery, ships, and flour mills. In 1886, Benjamin Holt of Stockton began manufacturing wheat harvesters. When his newer steam-powered tractors began sinking in the soft Delta soil, he developed revolving treads in 1904, and the Caterpillar tractor was born. Lumbering supplied wood for houses from the Gold Rush to the present, and in Gold Rush Sacramento in 1849, William P. Fuller started a business to paint them. "Western Made for Western Trade," proclaimed these "manufacturers of paints for every purpose."

Fish and fruit canning also remain important through such century-old, nationally known brands as Del Monte, named after the fabulous Monterey hotel, and Samuel Sussman, Gustav Wormser & Co. (S&W). As a great seaport, San Francisco attracted coffee roasters. James A. Folger began his "pioneer steam coffee and spice mills" in May 1850, (Austin H. and Reuben W.) Hills Brothers came in 1878, and Max J. Brandenstein & Co. (MJB) emerged in 1881. In that year, August Schilling & Co. split off from Folger's to specialize in spices.

What began as an attractive economic pursuit in the nineteenth century became a prime source of income in the twentieth. By the 1950s, almost 2 million bags per year made coffee the Port of San Francisco's largest commodity, amounting to over half of all imports in value. Ranking behind only New York and New Orleans in the United States, San Francisco produced one-twelfth of the world's ground coffee. Now the scent of roasting coffee along the waterfront is gone. Proctor & Gamble gobbled up Folger's in 1963, while Nestle S.A. of Switzerland got the latter two coffee producers in 1985.

Vigorously flourishing woolen manufacturers employed six thousand in 1880, including many Chinese, but the state still exported 80 percent of its wool crop. Niche marketing, such as

San Francisco's Levi Strauss & Co.'s 1873 patented, copper-riveted "501 jeans" set fashion for the next century. From the Gold Rush, Californians polished slabs of quartz gold for fine jewelry that still bedazzles. California's leather work matched its woolen blankets, Levi's jeans, and gold jewelry in worldwide esteem, but again a large percentage of quality hides left for manufacture elsewhere.

"THE CHINESE MUST GO!"

Capitalists, ever responsive to labor costs, sought to expand industry and agriculture where they could employ cheap Chinese labor. Workingmen resisted mightily.

On January 1, 1867, the SS *Colorado* began direct, scheduled mail steamer service with China and Japan. Far west from California, across the broad Pacific Ocean, companies imported the industrious, ambitious Chinese. Foremost they went to work on the Central Pacific Railroad, building east across the Sierra into Utah. Their skills made them desirable as urban laborers and farm harvesters. A congressional committee in 1878 announced that in the early 1860s, sixty-six hundred Chinese arrived annually; ten years later, the figure was thirteen thousand. It warned, "The Chinese population will, in the near future, exceed the male adult population of Americans," and found "even at present, it closely approximates the voting population." Unsurprisingly, wages dropped, jobs became scarce, and agitation grew against the Chinese.

In isolated, rugged Siskiyou County, a laboring man closed 1869 advising a friend in Rhode Island not to come to California "for this reason: The China labor is all the go now. The Chinamen work cheap & there is no call for white men, only experienced miners to oversee."

*At the turn of the twentieth century, Los Angeles Chinese children in tra-
ditional dress face a camera shyly—although the youngest is ready to
take on the world. As with all immigrant groups, most of the Chinese
who arrived were single men. Only a few of the small number of
women arrivals bore children. The Chinese Exclusion Act of 1882
choked off more from arriving. (Photograph by Warren C. Dickerson.)*

From the same era, unidentified children or friends of Chan Kiu Sing, a Los Angeles court interpreter and Methodist minister, pose in Western dress. After graduating from the University of Southern California, his son Spencer Chan became a movie actor, while in 1919 his daughter Caroline became a schoolteacher.

In 1882, a Watsonville woman vented against the Chinese: "My stock of patience, as you know," she wrote a Berkeley student, "is very limited. Next time I shall think twice before employing a denizen of the Flowery Kingdom to be my dish cloth wielder. I talk and talk and talk (how I do talk) to him and all I get from him is the most vacant and unknowing of Chinese stares with an occasional gleam of awakening intelligence. We can make bread and such and wash windows." Of course, she was speaking in English, and expected him to understand; if he had talked to her in Chinese, the "vacant stares" would have been on the other side.

In the cities Chinese workers expanded into local industries, capturing, among others, cigar and shoe manufacturing. The Chinese, making up one of every six workingmen in San Francisco, led laboring Irish and Germans to fear further cuts in wages. In 1877, Dennis Kearny led the San Francisco Workingmen with the slogan, "The Chinese Must Go!" To great cheers from California, Congress ultimately responded in 1882 with the Chinese Exclusion Act, not repealed until 1943 during World War II.

The Workingmen's Party and its allies controlled the Constitutional Convention that assembled in 1878 to revise the organic law of 1849, and voters ratified its work in 1879. Angry strictures denounced Chinese labor and provisions taxed rich corporations, reduced the power of the legislature, and restricted lobbying. The new constitution also reduced court costs, capped interest rates, regulated banks, and provided free schooling and textbooks. Denounced at the time for being the demagoguery of workingmen and farmers, the Constitution of 1879 is California's present organic law.

The Workingmen's electoral wave of victories swept in one supreme court justice, one of three railroad commissioners, eleven state senators and twenty-six assemblymen. In the Bay

A trade card printed in New York City's notorious Irish slum, Five Points, reaches across the continent to stereotype Chinese as launderers. Aroused by greedy corporations that paid low wages and supported Chinese immigration, Dennis Kearny's supporters in the San Francisco's Workingmen's Party dominated the 1878 state Constitutional Convention.

City, Workingmen made the Reverend Isaac Kalloch mayor of San Francisco, and he brought personal feuding and violence with him. In 1879, the opposition San Francisco *Chronicle* detailed Kalloch's past political, economic, and social indiscretions in "A course of Lust, Fraud, and Hypocrisy," that had given the red-haired Baptist minister the nickname of "The Sorrel Stallion."

Kalloch replied in kind. In a style of journalism not current today, he described his opponent as "the spawn of the brothel, conceived in infamy, dandled in the lap of a prostitute, bastard progeny of a whore, hybrid monster from hell, one Charley De Young." The next day, editor De Young, known equally for vituperation, blackmail, and shooting, ambushed and badly wounded Kalloch. The next year, Kalloch's son returned the compliment, killing De Young.

Politics were equally as sordid as journalism. Through the rest of the decade, and elsewhere in the United States as exemplified by Boss William Marcy Tweed's Tammany Hall Ring in New York City, political bosses ruled cities. Foremost in the San Francisco machine was Democratic "Blind Boss" William Buckley. Yet, in 1891, Republicans put in boss Daniel Burns. Corruption was an equal-opportunity operation.

ALWAYS WORKING TO GET AHEAD

For common folk, the majority of all Californians from laborers to professionals, life was one of manual toil and creative confusion. A woman remarked in 1875. "There is such a sort of hurry and excitement in the way people live here—and such a rush of business and speculation that anything is forgotten as soon as it happens." This sparked risk-taking enterprise.

99

Those who provided needed mercantile, financial, and delivery services to city dwellers and farmers worked as hard as their customers. In September 1869, Wells, Fargo & Co.'s Express agent at Gilroy wrote, "My salary is $100 per month out of which I have to pay my own board. Next week Expresses will be put on twice a day and then I will have to work from 6 in the morning until 9 at night, Sundays included."

In small, rural Descanso, San Diego County, population one hundred, a shopkeeper penned on May 1, 1878: "I am up by sunrise [5 A.M.] My breakfast is finished and the store in order by six or a little after, and even with this, people have come while I was in bed or at breakfast! However, few come after three or four in the afternoon."

An early twentieth-century traveling salesman, based in Butte County and specializing in "McConnon's Remedies, Flavoring Extracts, Spices, Toilet Articles, Etc.," reported on his own set of difficulties: "It costs 50 cents for horse hay a night and 50 cents per meal. I carry barley. It is hard for a beginner to get people to buy, and they are without money and far apart, but sometimes I sell $10 a day and ½ is mine."

Individual letters tell of a harder life for wage-earners. The foreman of the Puget Sound Lumber Company's yard in Fresno complained in 1880: "I'll be darned if a fellow can ever get ahead working for wages. I am getting $15 a week, but what does it amount to? I have to pay $6 a week for my board, and $2 for my washing and 25 cents for bath, and once in a while, have a shake down with the Spanish girls. So you see, I get left behind."

A decade later, in March 1890, a San Franciscan wrote a Connecticut friend about his life. He was "painting houses in side and out. I work 9 hours a day and get $2.50 per day," and "can live on that." To pleas that he return, as the forty-niners

Two gaunt horses stand ready to haul a load of sawn planks out of the San Bernardino Mountains. A full load provides an occasion for the family, dressed in their best, to go to town. Ingeniously chained davits keep tension on the boards to prevent shifting.

said forty years previously, "I should rather be here than East," for "this is a fine country," even if, "they work here harder than they do East."

Such wages were better than nothing. By 1890, five transcontinental railroads, the Great Northern, Northern Pacific, Central Pacific, Southern Pacific, and Santa Fe linked Pacific Coast economies to the east. Additionally, after December 1887, the Southern Pacific ran through from Portland, Oregon, to San Diego. Crisis in one place spread to all the others. "I wish you could see the idle men out here in this country," one expectant laborer wrote from Sacramento in December 1892 as the Panic of 1893 approached, "and they can't get any work at all."

The Panic of 1893 was the first national depression to hit California. Manufacturing and agriculture stalled, prices for grain and fruit hit lows, mercantile firms failed, and unemployment grew. Of 284 Golden State banks, six national, nineteen state, and two savings banks closed—a national number that only Kansas exceeded. Of these twenty-seven, five national banks, twelve commercial banks, and one savings bank later reopened, making the loss only 3 percent of the state's financial institutions.

Panics received their name from frenzied behavior. Economic downturns contracted the money supply, leading customers to run to withdraw bank deposits. Deposits were not federally insured, as they have been since the 1930s, so those who arrived first received their money; latecomers lost all savings. For purposes of public relations, the stock market crash of 1929 and resulting crisis was labled a depression rather than a panic. As the severeness of the Great Depression became legendary, the lower end of economic cycles became recessions, and even that is now obscured.

ENTERPRISING CALIFORNIANS

Women's work certainly was no easier than men's and harder to find. One of the few respectable jobs for women played on their domesticity. Keeping borders, one told friends in 1875, was "the easiest and best thing I could do." Here is how Fanny A. Grove described the practice at 605 Ellis Street: "I have considerable company and all the cooking for three meals a day and most of the dishwashing—and [her niece] Fanny and I do our washing and ironing too, as well as much of the cleaning. I have a Chinaman once in two or three weeks to wash windows, and clean the halls."

Of course, the burden of work fell on Ms. Grove, and she complained: "I have lost twenty-two pounds in weight since coming into my house." Three days later, she added, "My letters have to be written by piecemeal—I am so often interrupted. [We] are now waiting for the different roomers to come in, so that we can turn off the gas and go to bed."

New areas of woman's work met resistance for reasons as old as mankind. In 1896, a Sacramento doctor closed a letter, remarking that his wife, fearful of young, attractive competition, "objects to my having a 'typewriting girl,' so this work is done by myself." More significantly, enterprising women entered the work force, gaining praise for their clerical abilities. In mid-June 1889, the San Francisco *Examiner* reported "a change was made in the auditing department of Wells, Fargo & Co., the positions of eight young men being filled by six young women. The change was made because the young men, whose work was of a purely mechanical character, indulged in too much fun, disturbing the expert accountants employed with them." Though the company reduced the work force by two, "the change has proved to be very much for the better," noted

103

VOTE FOR THE WOMAM SUFFRAGE AMENDMENT,

NOVEMBER 3, 1896.

WHY?

Who pay taxes? Men and women.

Who make the laws governing taxation? Men.

Who may say how tax-money collected from men and women shall be used? Men only.

May not a capable woman who runs her own farm or other business have a vote in elections that concern her interests as much as those of any man?
No, but the most incapable man in her employ may.

May not a woman of education, who understands the questions of the day, vote?
No, but the most ignorant of men may.

May not women who teach the boys in our schools vote? No, but the boys they instruct, when 21, may vote.

Therefore, vote for the Suffrage Amendment because it is just and right.

WOMAN SUFFRAGE STATE HEADQUARTERS:
563, 564, 565 Parrott Building,
San Francisco.
[OVER]

Although the first petitions for woman's suffrage arrived at the state legislature in 1870, victory did not come until 1911, when California became the sixth state to grant that right. In the fiercely fought 1896 election, supporters argued, "No woman can vote for her own political freedom. She earnestly appeals to the justice and chivalry of every man in California who casts a ballot on November 3rd." Less than a century later, in 1992 Diane Feinstein became the first woman to represent California in the United States Senate.

the journalist, "one of the officials remarking that now work can be done quietly and accurately."

If money could be made in some enterprise, a Californian was there. The great wheat county of Yolo saw two such ventures. In 1864, (William and George) Hume, (Andrew) Hapgood & Co. established the Pacific Coast's first salmon cannery in Washington, where Hannah Rines got her start. A few years later in 1870, David Quincy Adams, one of the few who had struck it rich in the mines, turned to a new crop. He built a canal to irrigate one hundred and fifty acres of alfalfa brought from Chile, which is today the strain grown in Northern California.

In nearby Sonoma County, L.C. Byce in 1879 launched Petaluma as the chicken capital of the world through inexpensive, effective incubators and brooders. Further south, a Central Valley observer remarked that jackrabbits were twice the size of Eastern ones. "These rabbits are as thick as grass hoppers in places," he observed, and "will sit on their hind quarters and look right straight at you. They look comical with their great long ears 8 or 10 inches in length. They are nice eating. Some men make good wages killing them for the San Francisco market."

More widespread animal husbandry involved sheep-raising. One new migrant to Red Bluff said in 1870, "Keeping sheep is the easiest way of making money, they say, for it costs nothing to keep them, only for a man to take care of them." However, there were social costs. One herder wrote from San Mateo, two years later, "I have been right with the sheep for nearly three years and seventy miles from any town or society." From Delano in 1876, a woman wrote, "John started to the Mountains [and] will be gone three or four weeks. [Her eight-year old son] Hiram and I are alone now." Ultimately, in the late nineteenth century, Basques took over the business,

About 1907, a confident shepherd, alone but for two dogs, stands watch at San Pedro. Throughout the West, Basques came to herd sheep. (Photograph by Warren C. Dickerson.)

clashed with cattlemen, but spread throughout the West to become remarkable sheepherders.

The Central Valley wife continued, "Business is very dull. Sheep and Wool very low. There has been a good many sheep sold for 75 cents per head and good mutton sheep have been sold at $1.00–$1.25 per head. Some of our wool has been sold for 15½ cents per pound. That is rather discouraging, but we must live in hopes of better times. If we can manage to keep what we have got and have plenty of Range for them, we will come out all right in course of a year or two." However, drought this decade, coupled with overstocking and over-grazing the land, curtailed sheep ranching.

FARMERS UNITE

In the country, farmers sought strength in numbers. In 1867, Oliver H. Kelly founded the Grange in the national capital and watched these "Patrons of Husbandry" farmers' cooperatives spread across the United States. In Chicago, for instance, in 1872, the Grangers Montgomery Ward & Co. became the first mail-order house in the country. It encouraged buying clubs, where a local group gathered to purchase items in bulk, and therefore gain discounts, and advertised, "Grangers supplied by the Cheapest Cash House in America." Although the department store closed in January 2001, large grange halls still serve as community meeting centers in many California towns.

El Dorado County led California into the cooperative grange movement on August 10, 1870, with Pilot Hill Grange, No. 1. Of twenty-nine charter members, ten were women, as they had equal rights with men. In Martinez, Grangers built a nineteen-hundred-foot wharf, plus appropriate holding warehouses, for the shipping of their grain. Through the 1880s, California was the wheat producer of the world; it produced the most wheat of anywhere, and supplied it worldwide.

Dr. John Strentzel, president of the Grangers Warehouse and Business Association of Contra Costa, who grew a thousand varieties of fruits, nuts, and grapes, (and who later was the father-in-law of naturalist John Muir), dedicated the pier in September 1876. Farmers could now "mass their surplus at a central point, whence it can be moved at a moment's notice to any available market." With no middleman, "the producer can meet the capitalist." Just as Grangers did in Chicago with Montgomery Ward, Californians formed a similar cooperative Grangers' Business Association and in 1875 also incorporated a bank. Their joint efforts quickly saved $500,000 in charges for grain bags, and $3 million in freight charges.

107

Raising wheat, though, was a constant, time-consuming struggle in spite of the rich land. One farmer wrote from Antelope, Yolo County, in August 1870, "Grain threshed and in the corral. There were 4,100 bushels of wheat and over 1,300 of barley. You know that is about 600 bushels more than I expected. They were three days threshing." After all that work, he mourned that the market was down, "Wheat is only worth $1.60 and barley $1 [per 100 pounds]."

At Grand Island in Colusa County, grower John Brown described his congenial harvesters in 1879, roving from farm to farm, cutting and stacking from fifteen to twenty-five acres per day. "There are three classes of people represented," he wrote, "Caucasians, Mongolians & Redmen or Indians." Descriptions followed: "There are four of us Caucasians; Two Indians; One Chinaman (Cook). There is a Rancheria of Civilized Indians of 76 or 100 about a quarter a mile from here. They are splendid hands in the harvest field."

Unfortunately, drought became all too common. In June 1888, a Fresno observer remarked, "The grain crop is nearly a total failure," and a revealing remark followed: "It don't seem natural to have to depend on irrigation for a crop." His conclusion? "I can never content myself to settle down in such a terribly dry place as this is, no how," and he headed off to the perpetually wet Washington Territory.

New bulk crops then caught the attention of farmers. "Every day, there are car loads of apricots passing through here [Fresno] to the San Francisco market, from Los Angeles County," one man said. By 1890, refrigerated carload lots of deciduous and citrus fruit, potatoes, asparagus, and other California vegetables traveled regularly across the continent to Chicago, Cleveland, Buffalo, Boston, and New York.

ABATING ECOLOGICAL DISASTER

In California, mining continued to be an important industry. Chinese miners performed most of the low-capital placer mining, scavenging worked-over claims. In general, though, in the 1860s mining became big business, demanding incorporated companies with funds raised through stock sales. Hardrock mines, in a band reaching from Nevada through Tuolumne counties, tunneled thousands of feet through the earth. They employed hundred of miners, but no Chinese were allowed.

Placer or gravel mining also expanded greatly. The foremost technique was hydraulic mining, a California invention. Monitors, huge iron nozzles that controlled a high-pressure stream of water, blasted away packed gravel hills to recover a few cents of gold per cubic yard. Built by miners, in June 1878, the world's first long distance telephone went into operation in Nevada County. The Ridge Telephone Company connected fifty-eight miles of gravel pits to reservoirs to quickly regulate water pressure for hydraulicking.

Of course, all that dirt and gravel had to go somewhere, and downriver it went, raising the river's overflow plain up to a hundred feet and flooding the surrounding farmland. Fruit and grain farmers suffered mightily and fought back in court. In 1884, Judge Lorenzo Sawyer banned unrestrained hydraulic mining, ruling that miners had to trap sediment. Local Anti-Debris Associations, and later the state Debris Commission, undertook to enforce the ban on river dumping, while the Ridge Telephone now also warned of coming inspections. Gradually, streams became cleaner.

As an example of the damage caused by silted rivers, on March 11, 1886, the City of Stockton brought suit against the Boston Hydraulic Gold Mining Company, incorporated in

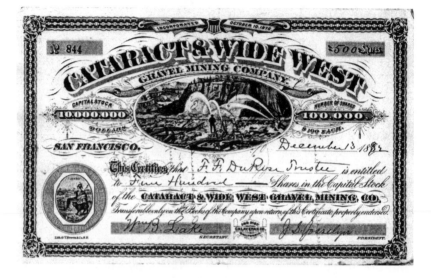

Hydraulic mining allowed the cheap extraction of small amounts of gold from huge amounts of gravel. Water jets blasted away hillsides, producing ecological disaster as rocky tailings ruined prime downstream farmland. Here African American artist and lithographer Grafton T. Brown details the miners' flumes, pipes, and monitors (nozzles) at work.

Massachusetts. It owned one thousand acres near Jenny Lind in Calaveras County, and used 13,500 gallons of water a minute at a two hundred-foot vertical pressure to blast away hillsides.

Beginning in the summer of 1849, the city argued, all vessels reached Stockton, but "that since the year 1862 the navigation of said streams [Calaveras and San Joaquin Rivers which join in Stockton] has become seriously impaired by deposits of 'tailings' therein from hydraulic mines, so that now the city of Stockton can only be reached from the bay of San Francisco by steamers or vessels of deep draught during high states of water."

The troubles then became worse, Stockton alleged. Hydraulic mining "attained great dimensions about the year 1876," the city charged, and tailings were "now filling up and raising the beds and channels of said San Joaquin River and Stockton and Mormon channels." Resulting sandbars caused the shipping channels "to overflow their banks and submerge large portions of the city of Stockton, including the streets," the city averred, resulting in "damage, discomfort and intolerable annoyance to the owners."

The city declared it could gain no redress in law and asked the court to stop this mining. It alleged that all charged with this mere misdemeanor would be "difficult and generally impossible to convict." Not only did hydraulickers maintain "great influence," but "a majority of the people of Calaveras County," regarded "the wrongful acts hereinabove complained of as constituting no offense." Furthermore, Stockton stated, "real and speculative profits" of hydraulicking outweighed "all the prosecutions and penalties of the law." Essentially, mining counties did not care about downstream farmlands.

By the end of the century a new type of mining, deep gravels, caught the attention of capitalists. Wendell P. Hammon abandoned fruit trees to develop huge dredges to harvest

111

The J.D. Peters, *a 206-foot sternwheeler built in 1889, leaves Stockton about the time of World War I. Into the 1930s, California rivers carried huge amounts of produce and freight, as well as large numbers of passengers.*

Yuba #14

In about 1918, the business end of the Marysville-built Yuba Consolidated Gold Fields bucket-line Dredge No. 14 faces the camera. These huge buckets could scoop up to ⅔ cubic yard of gravel at a time from 120 feet below the surface. The take? Only 0.6 percent of a troy ounce per cubic yard. If gold were $400 an ounce, this would be $2.40. Moving in their own ponds, these dredges churned the land for miles.

equally gigantic gravel fields in Butte and Yuba Counties. The dredges scooped up gravel from the front, screened it for gold, and dumped the tailings out the rear, moving along their own ponds. Behind they left huge fields of cobbles.

Up country in the Sierra foothills in the 1870s, Samuel Knight at Sutters Creek, Amador County, and Lester Pelton in Nevada City, invented efficient waterwheels to provide unlimited cheap energy, while six thousand miles of miners' ditches became the foundation for Pacific Gas & Electric's hydraulic energy system.

BEAUTY FOR THE FUTURE: FROM BIG TREES TO YOSEMITE VALLEY

Widespread mining-based landscape devastation coupled with California's unparalleled natural beauty brought visitors for the scenery and champions to preserve it. Golden State tourism gave birth to the preservation of Yosemite Valley, the Big Trees, and the National Parks system.

Beginning in the mid-1850s, travelers rushed to see the glories of California. James Mason Hutchings became the foremost promoter of nature through his *California Magazine* (1856–1861), and published compilations for thirty years afterwards. His love and residence was Mariposa County's Yosemite Valley. From the 1870s on, Scot John Muir, an indefatigable hiker with an inventive mind, was best associated worldwide with that remarkable valley and environmental conservation.

Money to be made from California tourism brought the first protection to Yosemite Valley. In 1864, Israel W. Raymond, an old California steamship company representative, proposed a novel suggestion to Senator John Conness, "California's sober senator." Raymond asked that the federal government have the lands of that gorgeous, glaciated valley "granted for public use, resort and recreation," and be "inalienable forever."

The senator incorporated the steamboat man's language into his bill, which President Abraham Lincoln signed on June 30, 1864. Under its provisions, the state would become guardian of the valley, with eight commissioners, plus the governor, acting as overseers. Perceptive Frederick Law Olmsted, noted environmental landscape designer best known for New York City's Central Park, became the first chairman. In 1865, he wrote a farseeing report, essentially setting out the philosophy of the later National Parks system, but other commissioners suppressed it. Still, the commissioners worked to close out private claims within the valley and construct trails for hikers.

In 1872, the federal government established Yellowstone National Park, declaring the 2.2 million acres, mostly in Wyoming, "free from injury or spoliation," and in 1879, created a Division of Forestry. Californians turned to the latter and the General Land Office to protect the giant sequoia trees. Ironically, though logged into the early twentieth century, the lumber was not commercially valuable. In 1880, the land office offered limited restraints, leading U.S. Senator John F. Miller in 1881 to propose a sequoia national park to encompass all major groves. Crisis came when the Secretary of the Interior permitted loggers into the large stands of trees. However, editor George W. Stewart of the Visalia *Delta* turned the full eye of the press on such wanton destruction. His decade of fulmination brought victory on September 25, 1890. Congress created the Sequoia National Park.

Less than a week later, Yosemite National Park followed on October 1, 1890. It expanded boundaries to fifteen hundred square miles around the forty-eight square miles of the state-owned valley. As more people discovered the secluded paradise, the Commissioners allowed more logging, the plowing of pristine meadows to grow hay for the travelers' horses, and additional commercial ventures. Clamor commenced successfully for a national park. Even the "soulless Southern Pacific R.R. Co.," John Muir remarked, "helped nobly in pushing the bill for this park through Congress." In 1905, Muir's friendship with railroad magnate Edward Henry Harriman proved crucial in the close passage of the bill whereby the state relinquished its claims to Yosemite Valley. Unified national administration came on August 2, 1906.

Appropriately, the Army, which had for a century scientifically investigated the West, guarded the new national park. Longtime commander Colonel Harry C. Benson vigorously defended Yosemite from encroachment and built the current system of trails into the back country. From 1903 to 1916, black cavalry units, the famed Buffalo Soldiers, patrolled Yosemite and Sequoia. In 1916, the National Parks Service emerged to continue stewardship.

On June 4, 1892, John Muir led the formation of Sierra Club to act as a civil guardian for Yosemite, using popular and political clout as needed. Members would "explore, enjoy, and render accessible the mountain regions of the Pacific Coast," and especially "enlist the support and cooperation of the people and the government in preserving them."

The gregarious Muir served as president of the San Francisco-based organization until 1914, unsuccessfully battling to prevent the flooding of Yosemite's twin valley, Hetch Hetchy, for San Francisco's water supply. The John Muir Trail serves as his best memorial, running two hundred and sixty miles along the crest of the Sierra from Yosemite to Mount Whitney, with long portions above thirteen thousand feet. Beginning in 1990, every April 21 has been "John Muir Day."

The Southern Pacific, a regular advertiser in the *Sierra Club Bulletin*, promoted tourism in Yosemite National Park since its

Since the 1850s, the gorgeous Yosemite Valley has charmed tourists. A party casually poses in front of Yosemite Falls, circa 1875.

1890 beginning. In 1909, for instance, round trip rates by railroad and continuing stagecoach "over the crisp, crackling road that exhilarates pulse and brain," were $22.35 from San Francisco and $31.20 from Los Angeles. "Wheelmen," as bicyclists were known, also made the grand valley a destination, and, as one guide book of the time remarked, "the sensible stage horses no longer fear them." Even in winter, Yosemite was attractive. Arriving was "a trip to fairyland," the railroad declared, "where snowballing goes without saying." A 1926 brochure celebrating the opening of the All-Year Highway on July 31, simply called the incomparable valley, "California's All-Year Playground."

It was. In 1899, out of 4,500 valley visitors, Mr. and Mrs. David A. Curry welcomed 290 to their tent campground; in 1907, 1,800 camped with them out of 8,000 tourists to Yosemite. In 1922, the Currys' number reflected the year, 22,000, and Mother Jennie

Curry offered 650 tents at $4 per person, including meals. A running joke declared that beans were the staple food. After the main course one evening in August 1925, Roy, an otherwise unidentified camper wrote, "we were asked if we wanted some strawberries." Of course he did, but he only realized the joke when "a plate of beans appeared."

At that time, another brochure remarked, "Since the National Parks were opened to automobiles in 1913, Yosemite has been the mecca of the mountain motorist. In recent years, three out of every four visitors to Yosemite have motored in." The year 1926 saw 274,000 travelers; with the new highway in full operation, 1927 brought 490,000 tourists. In 1970, 80 percent of visitors were overnighters; now, of the 3.5 million who annually tour the fragile valley, 80 percent are in and out during the day. Vast flooding of the Merced River in 1997 led the National Parks Service to reduce the number of cars and reconfigure accommodations in order to keep this natural treasure available to all.

BLACK BART AND OTHER OUTLAWS

While Workingmen's agitation rocked San Francisco, the interior of California also saw violence. High-cost hardrock and hydraulic mining corporations now produced the gold, excluding individual miners. The Mother Lode band of mining towns, along the twentieth century's north-south Highway 49, declined without the infusions of corporate payrolls. Wealth flowed to the lowlands, where residents turned to raising wheat on the flatlands, and fruit in the foothills. Wells, Fargo & Co.'s express still carried gold out from the hills and gold coin back, and its green, iron-strapped treasure boxes proved tempting.

For twenty years, from the mid-1860s to the mid-1880s, stagecoach robbing became a growth industry. Wells, Fargo & Co., which contracted with local carriers to transport its express, averaged twenty-five holdups a year, losing $30,000 annually—but it also helped secure 225 convictions over a fourteen-year time span.

On July 25, 1875, a legend appeared on a steep, lonely stage road in Calaveras County. A masked figure in a linen duster holding the ever-essential shotgun and a backup 16-shot rifle, kindly asked the stage driver to throw down the treasure box. A safe inside the coach under the back seat escaped molestation. For the next eight years, this loner ranged through northern California into southern Oregon, and with a fine sense of humor, taunted Wells Fargo. The third verse was certainly truthful:

Let come what will I'll try it on
My condition can't be worse
And if there's money in that box
'Tis money in my purse.

The mystery man, a frustrated writer, signed the verses, "Black Bart, The Po8." In twenty-nine attempted stagecoach robberies, Black Bart's one failure came on July 13, 1882, when shotgun messenger George Hackett successfully defended $23,000 in treasure and sent the outlaw scurrying.

Black Bart's career came to an end in 1883, eight years after it began, when he returned to the scene of his first crime and matched wits with a stage safe holding $4,700. On November 3, 1883, the outlaw escaped with the treasure—he was hurried along after a friend of the driver arrived on the scene with a rifle. Black Bart obtained a gold bar, but dropped a tell-tale handkerchief that his laundry had identified with the mark, F.X.O.7.

119

A gentlemanly but misunderstood outlaw looks as dignified as his situation will allow, after being apprehended by police. Although Charles Boles ("Black Bart") robbed at least twenty-eight stagecoaches carrying Wells Fargo gold between 1875 and 1883, he was really a literary man. As proof, he left doggerel at crime scenes signed, "Black Bart, the Po8." (Courtesy of Wells Fargo.)

Wells Fargo Chief Detective James B. Hume called on the best, private detective Harry Morse. He ran the mark through ninety-one San Francisco laundries, tracing it to an elegantly dressed loner, Charles Boles. Black Bart was imprisoned until early 1888—and then he disappeared into the unknown.

By 1886, Detective Hume concluded that stagecoach robbery was "a thing of the past." Railroad extension and a paper money-order system killed it off, as large sums of gold no longer traveled by coach. In 1886, fifteen stage holdups cost Wells Fargo only $300, leaving Hume to comment dryly, "This, of course, leaves a very narrow margin for the robbers." However, the "higher grade of criminal talent," Hume remarked, merely plotted train robberies, especially throughout the Southwest. Wells Fargo suffered twenty-three attacks between 1887 and 1891.

A string of California train robberies grew out of a titanic clash in Tulare County between the mighty Southern Pacific Railroad and armed Southern-born squatters, who had flouted public authority since the Civil War. By 1879, sixty thousand acres of even numbered township sections made a prosperous, irrigated area of small farms. The railroad, though, claimed alternating square-mile sections authorized as its government land grant. As policy, the national government encouraged development all along a railroad right-of-way by keeping half the land in the public domain. By alternating ownership of sections, it blocked huge contiguous strips. Speculators, of course, took advantage of the title dispute and rushed to occupy lands claimed by the railroad.

On May 11, 1880, a U.S. Marshal faced the Settlers' Grand League at Mussel Slough. In the confrontation between federal authority protecting railroad rights and the squatters, seven died. By the end of the year, though, the Southern Pacific granted payment terms that gave most squatters legal title to their land. Appropriately, the satirical magazine *Wasp* on August 19, 1882, published a biting cartoon titled "The Curse of California," depicting Mussel Slough as just one of many properties, including steamboats, newspapers, and legislatures, in the clutches of a gigantic railroad octopus.

Beginning in 1889, allegedly to avenge "the Mussel Slough robbery" of squatters' land, Chris Evans and John Sontag attacked Southern Pacific trains, killing four people in the process. In spite of their claims, and strong Tulare County support, the robbers did not practice Robin Hood-style social banditry. After the third California robbery in 1891 and before the fourth in 1892, Evans with John Sontag's brother George, robbed a train in Wisconsin, and the Sontag brothers hit one in Minnesota.

Law enforcement eventually killed, or captured and convicted the train robbers, but the Tularians won the public relations battle. Popular opinion held that a greater outlaw existed. Although the Southern Pacific had legal title to the lands, when Frank Norris published his powerful novel, *The Octopus*, in 1901, the grasping, monopolistic railroad was seen as evil. The culmination of this tale of widespread gouging of wheat growers was the massacre at Mussel Slough. The second half of the nineteenth century and California's 1.5 million people indeed belonged to the railroad.

CHAPTER IV

The Pace of Life Quickens
(1900–1940)

The early years of the new century challenged Californians in every aspect of their lives. The government threw off railroad control to become more democratic politically, but World War I drew California and the nation into the world's problems. The automobile and airplane brought mobility, while a diversified agricultural economy encouraged a multitude of different newcomers. As population grew dramatically, Los Angeles, San Francisco, and other urban areas dealt with everything from earthquakes and water-supply disputes to retail banking and labor strife.

When Prohibition came in the 1920s, Protestant Midwest migrants in Los Angeles supported it; while European immigrant San Francisco did not. Regardless, rum runners did well everywhere. Yet, the prosperity and giddiness of the 1920s collapsed into the economically crippling Great Depression of the 1930s. However, cheap movies provided relief, fantasy, and entertainment.

Through it all, life went on. Parents raised children, the next generation. In 1915, a father wrote his son, "Have you had any fights of late? Remember you are not to start a fight, but

At 5:12 A.M. on April 18, 1906, San Franciscans had an early-morning wake-up call with an earthquake measuring 8.25 on the Richter scale. Even worse than the quake were the three days of fire that followed, which destroyed the oldest part of the city: everything east of Van Ness Avenue. Curiosity and almost a "party" mentality prevailed as San Franciscans closely watched flames devour their city.

In the new twentieth century, Pasadena experienced a revival in all the fine arts. This circa-1910 art shop illustrates the refined, cultured, baroque taste of the period. (Photograph by Warren C. Dickerson.)

when it is started you are to do as 'Best you can.' The best man does not always win, but to be in the right at least helps." Two years later came the advice, "As to the Calhoun boy, I think with a little coaching Herman can whip him. Just drill into his mind that he can do it and tell him the way to fight that kind of a bully is to wade in and hit as often as fast as he can and not to give him the time to get straight on his feet." Later he wrote, "I laughed at the way Herman was trying to 'swear,' and it took me back to the time when I was likely about his age and we were saying about the same things, for instance, 'you son of a bit your finger off' during the war."

PROGRESSIVE POLITICS

By the turn of the twentieth century, San Francisco, "the cool, gray city of love" of poet George Sterling, had had enough of corrupt bossism, while the state grew tired of railroad dominance. What was the Southern Pacific Railroad? A character from the Frank Norris novel *The Octopus* (1901) answered:

> "They swindle a nation of a hundred million and call it Financiering; they levy a blackmail and call it Commerce; they corrupt a legislature and call it Politics; they bribe a judge and call it Law; they hire blacklegs to carry out their plans and call it Organization; they prostitute the honor of a state and call it Competition."

San Francisco saw brief reform in the 1890s under Mayors Adolph Sutro, who actually campaigned in 1894 upon the platform, "The Octopus Must Be Destroyed," and James D. Phelan. Yet, a worse change came in 1901 when Abe Ruef, "the Curly Boss," gained city control through his Union Labor Party.

Blatant corruption marked his administration, leading to years of graft trials of high city officials beginning in 1906.

One of the prosecutors was a former Teamsters' Union lawyer, Hiram Johnson. As the Republican nominee for governor of California in 1910, Johnson campaigned in a red roadster Locomobile calling for moral regeneration. He represented "the great moral masses" against "the corrupt but powerful few," and specifically vowed to "kick the Southern Pacific out of politics." The railroad fought back, considering Johnson more "loco" than his car.

Johnson carried the state in what the San Francisco *Chronicle* called "a triumph of insurgency," and 1911 proved it. California became the sixth state to grant women the right to vote. When the state legislature convened, the chaplain declared, "Give us a square deal for Christ's sake." The legislature responded nobly with acts for participatory democracy and aid for the workingman. Particularly groundbreaking were three enactments that allowed the people to participate directly in government. The initiative, referendum, and recall respectively allowed the people to propose legislation, approve or reject legislative acts, and remove corrupt elected officials.

These populist expressions have played an important role in California's recent history. Current and continued legislative deadlock has made the initiative very powerful. For instance, before 1978, law did not restrict property tax rates. In 1978, Proposition 13 set taxes at 1 percent of market value and allowed a 2 percent annual increase. Property taxes dropped by half. Once sold, the county assessor appraised the property at current market value. Proposition 184 in 1994 caught the public mood for "law and order." A small criminal element committed most of the crime; jail was no deterrent. The "three strikes" initiative made a life sentence mandatory for a third conviction.

Proposition 209 in 1997 banned preferences (affirmative action) for minority groups. On October 7, 2003, Gray Davis became the first California governor to be deposed.

For labor, this 1911 legislature enacted workmen's compensation, and an eight-hour day for women, the first in the nation. The next legislature in 1913 went further. It regulated child labor, imposed factory inspections, and instituted a minimum wage for government contracts. Furthermore, with their new franchise, women's clubs dominated legislation on moral issues, replacing racetrack, gambling, liquor, and brothel interests, leading to bans or curtailment of vice.

Governor Johnson, for his part, joined Teddy Roosevelt in 1912 as vice president on the Bull Moose ticket. Their Progressive Party would "Pass Prosperity Around." For Johnson, government existed to "make men better rather than to make men richer." However, Democratic professor Woodrow Wilson won the presidential prize, and Governor Johnson turned his attention back to the Golden State. In California, he reformed the bureaucracy, replacing patronage with professionalism. In the 1916 election, Progressives now did well among laboring Catholic immigrants, and this alliance would re-emerge in 1932 to allow Franklin D. Roosevelt to carry the state.

THE GREAT WAR BANISHES INNOCENCE

America's 1917 entry into World War I shocked the now over 3 million Californians out of complacency. Historians have compared the 1850s Gold Rush to a war after gold-seekers left ·home to make California a land of young, single men. Now, seventy years later, native-born Californians would experience a real war. Many, for the first time, found themselves suddenly a long way from home, and realized that California, indeed, was part of a wider world.

World War I brought a rush of patriotism, as well as denunciation of all things German or Communist. This 1917 San Francisco school class of thirty-two children displays five American flags (as well as five books, five dolls, and one teddy bear).

"The martial spirit here" in the McKittrick oil fields, one man wrote, "is very high and as a rule the boys are all 'Rarin' to go.'" As they left, they made arrangements for those at home. A Californian wrote "Dear Pa," that he had "assigned $15 per month of my wages [half] to be sent to you."

The Army quickly established an offshore recruiting depot at San Francisco. "I am over on Angel Island," a new soldier wrote in September 1917. "I joined the army Sunday before last. I guess about an average of fifty enlist here every day." Another observed crowded conditions at Fort McDowell that

December: "There is sure a good many Humboldt boys down here. There can't be many left around there who are in the draft age. So many men enlisted during the last few days that the recruiting station couldn't handle them all."

The Army presented new experiences as well as new opportunities. One Angel Island recruit added, "I went swimming in Frisco Bay to day [June 16] and like to froze to death." Another's observations revealed that the details of Army life are constant: "They are very short of uniforms in sizes over 36," he said, "so I haven't got mine yet, but expect to get it tomorrow." Furthermore, the Army never met a potato it wished to remain unpeeled. "Nearly all of the fellows have had to serve in the kitchen. They call them K.P.'s or "Kitchen Police," the new recruit explained. Still, the Angel Island facility could handle all: "The mess room seats 1800 men, but the grub and service is good."

Rationing and the war effort affected everyone. One civilian noted, "I am having to donate to the war a little—one days wages to the W.M.C.A. [Young Men's Christian Association, whose California operations began in 1853] and one dollar to the Red Cross." Its services were broader than expected. "A W.M.C.A. is certainly a great thing for a camp," a 1917 soldier remarked. "It affords all sorts of amusement, besides furnishing writing and reading material." This playfulness and innocence vanished when soldiers reached France, but the curiosity, enthusiasm, and freshness exhibited here won the day for American infantrymen.

CALIFORNIA'S POPULATION GROWS MORE DIVERSE

The twentieth century continued to add large numbers of tiles to the detailed population mosaic of California, and by 1920

130

In March 1918, the first case in the United States of "Spanish Influenza" appeared at a military post, and it would ultimately kill 600,000 Americans. The next month the flu reached San Quentin Prison and in October became epidemic in San Francisco. The city ultimately reported 30,000 cases resulting in 3,500 deaths—more than the revised total for the 1906 earthquake. "Wear a Mask and Save Your Life! A Mask is 99 Percent Proof Against Influenza," became the logic of a city law making them mandatory.

Los Angeles became the state's largest city. European exploration in the eighteenth century spanned the world, while steam transportation and industrialization in the nineteenth century moved people around, mixing up rural groups that had stayed homogeneous for centuries. California's diversity had emerged with the Gold Rush. The irresistible siren song of the Golden State called to all: Italians, Armenians, Japanese, Koreans, Sikhs, Mexicans, and Filipinos.

California was caught in an opposite but complementary "yin-and-yang situation." The Declaration of Independence declares that "all men are created equal," while the national

131

motto, E Pluribus Unum, demands "Out of many, One." This contentious, painful need for both popular unity and acceptance of diversity continues to mark the social life of the United States and California. In the Golden State, peoples' notions of racial purity, plus observed, perceived, and imagined differences between members of different groups, led to stereotypes—a printing term for a text unchangeably cast in lead—applied to all members of that group.

While this social situation could have led to an unyielding caste system, goodhearted men and women used the law to provide a wedge for societal acceptance. Often the federal courts, relying on the post-Civil War Civil Rights legislation and the Fourteenth Amendment, struck down the most restrictive state and municipal laws—most of which were directed against the Chinese. Such judicial activism led later generations to equal legal and social rights. Few areas of the world have experienced such a large and diverse immigration that has poured into the United States, nor, over a period of years, granted such broad rights to newcomers comprising such a large portion of the population.

Italians and Armenians

The Gold Rush brought a small, skilled Italian population, mostly from northern Italy, who settled in San Francisco and the Southern Mines. Amador County became a particular stronghold. In 1869, when Italy itself was not yet unified, immigrants, while gathering by region, all joined together to celebrate Discovery Day, 1492. Angelo Noce, a son of Genoa like the great Columbus, participated in that first parade. He lobbied nationally for a legal holiday, now called Columbus Day. In 1909, California obliged; Federal recognition came in 1971. Appropriately, in 1910, San Francisco's Montgomery Avenue, the 1870s diagonal continuation of Montgomery Street into North Beach, became Columbus Avenue.

A second wave of Italian immigration to the United States began in the 1880s, comprising mostly unskilled peasants. While the majority settled on the East Coast, some ventured west. In 1890, California gave residence to fifteen thousand, one-third in San Francisco. In 1910, the Bay City itself had seventeen thousand and in 1924, when Federal legislation cut immigration, forty-five thousand—the largest number of foreign-born ever in San Francisco up to that date. In many cases, the old-timers did not welcome the "uncivilized" newcomers, who, like the forty-niners before them, wished to make their fortunes and return to Italy. A majority did, residing only four years in the Golden State.

Skilled San Francisco Italians in 1849 began harvesting the bounty of the bay, and by the 1860s, they sold fish to the Chinese at a time when the Chinese had a good reputation as fishermen themselves. In 1905, four thousand Italians working at the trade made California the second-largest fishery in the United States. San Francisco supplied salmon and sardines; Los Angeles provided tuna. In 1916, Tomaso Castagnola took out a license to sell fresh shrimp and crab cocktails on San Francisco's Fisherman's Wharf. His successors still reel in huge catches of tourists.

Italians in California also participated in opera, banking, and sports. Food was a specialty. Italians opened famed restaurants and handled fresh vegetables—growing, wholesaling, and retailing them. In the early twentieth century, Del Monte and S&W canned produce became known nationwide.

Names of noted families just roll off the tongue: Alioto, Andronico, Argenti, Bacigalupi, Bandini, Belli, Bianchi, Casanova, Chichizola, Father Crespi, Daneri, Di Giorgio, Dimaggio, Fontana, Fugazi, Gallo, Ghirardelli, Giannini, Guasti,

Father Kino, Luisetti, Father Maraschi, Martini, Mazzera, Molinari, Mondavi, Musto, Father Neri, Noce, Paladini, Petrini, Pisanelli, Rocca, Rossi, Sartori, Sbarboro, Scatena, Splivalo, Tarantino, and Valentino.

Italians and other European immigrants created California's famous wine industry. In the late 1850s, the Hungarian Agoston Haraszthy avidly promoted California wines. Through the last half of the nineteenth century, his equally committed son Arpad and the able Charles Wetmore led vintners and trumpeted the quality of California wines. By 1890, the Golden State produced about 80 percent of the wine made in the United States, and the Italian Swiss Colony complex at Asti became world famous.

Many Armenians came along with the second wave of Italians, fleeing the genocide of their people carried out by the Turks between 1915 and 1921. Settling around Fresno, they grew figs, raisins, and flavorful pistachio nuts, which became a commercial crop in the 1970s. In 1894, California figs were sold in the East for the first time. George Deukmejian, Governor of California from 1983 to 1991, traces his roots to this Armenian group, which after the influx of immigration numbered about eighteen thousand by 1930.

Agricultural Expansion Encourages Further Immigration: East and South Asians

After the turn of the century, California's agriculture boomed due to the conversion of large landed estates into farming corporations and the spread of irrigation districts throughout the great Central Valley. In 1900, California boasted 5.5 million navel orange trees, and these golden globes spread Golden State fame worldwide. For more effective marketing, growers joined together in agribusiness cooperatives. One loud voice rather than tiny individual growers' whispers could proclaim the goodness of California oranges. In 1905, the California Fruit Growers' Exchange formed. Better known by its brand name, "Sunkist," by 1915, it had fifteen thousand members; employed thirty thousand laborers in Los Angeles, Orange, Riverside, San Bernardino, and Tulare Counties; and ultimately controlled 70 percent of the state's citrus market.

The Golden State, with a quarter of the nation's irrigated land, produced two hundred commercial crops, and by 1925 it was the source of almost 30 percent of America's canned and dried produce. In second place, New Jersey, the "Garden State," produced about 10 percent. Some well-known Californian staples include California raisins, table and wine grapes, figs, fruits, dates, avocados, melons, almonds, walnuts, rice, and cotton. Immigrants also contributed their native produce. J.B. Avila, a Portuguese immigrant from the Azores, introduced his local crop—the sweet potato.

For more than fifty years, Luther Burbank, the "Plant Wizard" of Santa Rosa, improved eight hundred strains of trees, crops, and flowers. Best known is the Burbank or "Idaho" potato, an 1871 creation. For instance, in October 1885, a San Francisco produce merchant wrote an Oregon farmer explaining that the potato market stood "very low," but stated, "Now it depends a great deal what kind Potatoes you have. If you have some choice Burbanks, those selling the best." Santa Rosa Plums and Shasta Daisies are other Burbank innovations.

"He does not create, but he guides nature in creating," a 1905 article in *Cosmopolitan* declared, picturing an apple tree with 526 varieties of fruit on it. "The Burbank experiments," the author windily enthused, "prove that the plant-world is plastic to human touch, and that we may shape it at our will." Yet, environment became all important. "California was made

135

for him and he for California." Again, the dream of Eden surfaced: "He needed its wonderful climate, its rich and varied soil, its undeveloped, limitless possibilities; and it needed him with his power to bring out the latent forces in nature."

The new, large-scale agriculture resembled industrial enterprise more than traditional farming. Such "factories in the fields," to appropriate leftist historian Carey McWilliams' imagery, demanded roving gangs of cheap contract labor. With the Chinese precedent, owners imported men from throughout the world. Farms played one ethnic group against another to keep workers from organizing together. However, conditions in the fields were poor. Unsurprisingly, during the 1930s California saw 135 agricultural strikes, half of the national total. Strikes involved both American Communists and immigrant labor. As each ethnic group moved up the economic scale, employers sought newcomers who would work for lower wages. In this manner, profit continued to contribute to the diversity of California. Some declared this to be a debasing "menace to the white race." Such fears were not limited to California. In 1922, the U.S. Supreme Court banned from citizenship all who were "not Caucasian."

The inability to attain citizenship did not stem the tide from the Far East, however. The Chinese Exclusion Act of 1882 did virtually stop that flow of immigration—until 1906. Under the provisions of the federal law, Chinese born in California who left to visit China were allowed to return. San Francisco served as the main port of entry, but the three-day fire following the 1906 earthquake destroyed all municipal records. Immigration officials, therefore, had no proof of birth, and the number of returning Chinese exploded astronomically. Each woman resident in San Francisco would have had to have given birth to eight hundred children. These illegal immigrants, of course, were the "Paper Sons," who matched wits with immigration officials on Angel Island to prove they had a legal right to be in California. Confined for months, their poignant poetry remains on the barracks walls. Perhaps fifty thousand Chinese found residence until the repeal of the Exclusion Act in 1943.

The wartime need for manpower led to the loosening of such restrictions. In 1942, the government naturalized large numbers of Chinese and Filipino men. The repeal of the Exclusion Act granted that right to all Chinese aliens, while Congress extended it to Filipinos and East Indians in 1946. Finally, in 1952, the McCarren-Walter Act deleted the word "white" from the 1790 Naturalization Law.

San Francisco remains the center of Pacific Coast Chinese culture. Herb Lee became the first Chinese police officer in 1957, marking the emergence of Chinese political power. In 1992, at the urging of the Organization of Chinese Americans, the post office issued the first Chinese (Lunar) New Year stamp; 2004 will complete the series of twelve zodiac animals.

In 1888, Japanese laborers began arriving. These were literate, skilled farmers who established families. By 1909, four thousand worked in canneries, ten thousand as railroad workers, and forty thousand in agriculture, where they produced 70 percent of California's strawberries. "Potato King" George Shima also made his agricultural mark, controlling ten thousand acres of crops. By 1940, Japanese farmers dominated the state's fresh produce market—their crops constituted 95 percent of California's green beans and celery, two-thirds of its tomatoes, and about 40 percent of onions and green peas.

On an individual level, immigrants could find acceptance, usually in domestic-service positions. A Berkeley student wrote in 1915, "We have a Jap cook now and I believe he is going to be splendid. He is so clean and nice looking." Such had been said of the Chinese sixty years before—until public

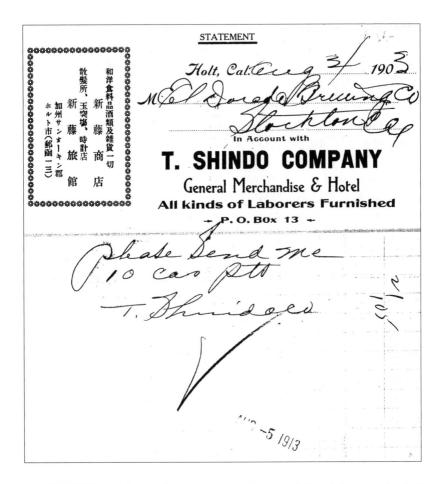

A 1913 billhead for a Japanese merchant and hotel keeper in hot Holtville, Imperial County, showed him also to be a labor contractor— probably for the area's well-known cantaloupe fields. In a system that began with Chinese immigrants and was especially galling to union farm workers, an employer would pay the crew boss a certain sum and let him pay workers individually.

opinion turned against them en masse, based on their increasing numbers.

Japanese success now sparked a similar fear, of what was called the "Yellow Peril." Many Caucasians had a strong desire to "Keep California White," in the words of Democratic Senator James D. Phelan's unsuccessful 1920 re-election campaign. According to Phelan, the very presence of the Japanese threatened "the future of the white race, American institutions, and western civilization." Restrictions were the result of this fear. In 1908, President Theodore Roosevelt negotiated a "Gentlemen's Agreement" with the Japanese government to limit immigration. In 1913, California fought the supposed Japanese menace through a law prohibiting aliens from owning land (the Alien Land Law), and restricting leases to three years. The Japanese simply switched ownership to their American-born children, until a 1920 initiative tightened restrictions against this "dreadful peril" from about one hundred thousand residents. Such constraints had the ironic effect of encouraging Japanese Americans born in California (Nisei) to succeed at all costs; in 1952, the California Supreme Court nullified this law.

In the first years of the new century, growers also turned to Korea and India, bringing in about 8,000 workers from each country. Koreans arrived educated and Christian, and by 1920 they cultivated 43,000 acres of rice around Willows. Ahn Changho, a 1902 immigrant to Los Angeles, founded the Korean National Association, which fought internationally against Japanese occupation of his homeland. The Indians, mostly Punjabi Sikhs, generally were migratory laborers who traveled from the cantaloupe and cotton fields of the Imperial Valley to pick the figs and grapes of Fresno, and to harvest rice above Sacramento. These men often married Mexican women to get around the Alien Land Law restrictions.

Between 1924 and 1965, the federal Immigration Restriction Act of May 26, 1924, prescribed quotas for various groups, based on the size of populations already here. In effect, it banned southern Europeans, Asians, and Mexicans. For their next labor force, growers turned to an American colony, the Philippines. By the 1930s, Stockton stood as the headquarters city for thirty thousand immigrants, mostly men, who comprised the largest number of Filipinos outside the islands. Radiating out from "Little Manila," their jobs followed the usual pattern; they worked in agriculture, fishing, and canning, and as domestics, dishwashers, and janitors. Strife arose in the Depression years when Filipinos intermarried with white women.

Now, something like nostalgia reigns in Stockton, as only three boarded-up buildings of "Little Manila" remain. At South El Dorado and East Lafayette Streets stands a union hall, where laborers fought asparagus growers. The (Jose) Rizal Social Hall also still exists. Named for an 1890s Philippine Independence martyr, it housed a ten-cent dance hall and gambling operations. A residential hotel for single male laborers remains as well.

However, the Filipino presence in California is far from vanished. A new "Manila Town" exists today in Daly City, which is now 54 percent Filipino. Since the 1980s, this population supplied 80 percent of the airport security screeners at the San Francisco, Oakland, and San Jose Airports.

AUTOMOBILES, AIRPLANES, AND OIL

Automobiles Arrive

Horses had carried mankind for millennia; surely an age of invention could speed travel. Through the 1890s, Europeans

With over 22 million cars today, California's love of the automobile is obvious. Around 1907, two cars climb Mount Roubidoux above Riverside. A woman drives the first, while the city Rain Cross emblem adorns the second's radiator. Note the readily available spare tires and the right-side steering wheel, European style. (Photograph by Warren C. Dickerson.)

and Americans developed horseless carriages. As 1900 dawned, eight thousand of them bucked and snorted around the United States. Surprisingly, about 40 percent each were steam or electric powered. Only 22 percent chugged around by gas engines. California covers a huge expanse of land; distances just seemed farther than any other place; people needed to get around fast.

The twentieth century brought the age of the automobile. The year 1900 saw the birth of the Auto Club of San Francisco

141

and its Southern California counterpart in Los Angeles, when only ten thousand cars existed in the entire country, with a mere thirteen in San Francisco itself. The next year, the clubs allied with the Good Roads movement, begun by bicyclists in the 1880s. Local road overseers, in charge of specific districts within each county, allegedly kept dirt roads in repair. Mud, ruts, and general deterioration caused enough headaches to drivers of high, horse-drawn farm wagons, but travel by bicycle and automobile was excruciating. Users demanded graded, paved roads. In these early years, not all were convinced of the auto's efficacy. Marin County banned them; it was "essentially a horse-keeping and horse-loving county."

In 1903, it would seem that a man would have had to be crazy to bet, and over drinks too, that he could make it across the United States behind the wheel of an automobile. However, Dr. Horacio Nelson Jackson, also known as the Mad Doctor, had the intrepid spirit of his namesake, the British admiral. On July 26, 1903, he departed from San Francisco's Palace Hotel in a twenty-horsepower, two-cylinder Winton, and sixty-three days later the "whizz wagon," according to journalistic license, chugged into New York City, completing the first transcontinental trip. The automobiles of the time were temperamental: Jackson spent nineteen days stopped, waiting for the railroad to deliver needed parts.

California finally issued uniform automobile operation regulations in 1905, while in 1908 Michigan, Henry Ford created an engine transmission, assembly line, and cheap price for the famed Model T. Ford sold 15 million of them through 1927, making cars an indispensable part of American life. In 1909, the society *Blue Book* of California listed names and addresses of all 18,328 registered owners of motor vehicles, with capitalist John D. Spreckels listed first. Currently, California contains over 22 million cars—with 5 percent of drivers not licensed.

A state bond passed in 1910 to finance new roads, and San Diego was the first county to take advantage of it. In 1912, seventeen years of work began on the north-south El Camino Real (Highway 101). California's southernmost county developed road-building techniques suitable for automobiles arriving for San Diego's 1915 Panama-Pacific Exposition that rejoiced at the completion of the Panama Canal. Often, long-distance roads followed railroad lines, as the railroads' topographical engineers had chosen the best transit lines. To prevent chaos on the roads, Cleveland, Ohio, introduced red and green traffic lights in 1914, and they spread nationally.

These new automobiles had their flaws. From 1915 comes the remark, "The truck is broken down and they are going to hitch the mules to it and take it to Bakersfield." In June 1917, a young woman wrote about a trip five miles down the coast to Santa Monica: "Returning, the 'machine' broke down and we came home in relays, tired but happy." The next day's diary entry read, "Remained at home to wear off effects of yesterday's picnic."

These "machines" consumed petroleum products. From March to May 1928, a young woman in Los Angeles regularly spent 93 cents for gas and 20 cents for oil every three days. Car repair continually drained her funds: Tighten brakes, 50 cents; rear axle, $10.50; buy, patch or change tire $7.50; lights and fix clutch, $1.10; gas tank fixed, $2.75; and fix carburetor, $2.85. Service stations sprang up to help such travelers. "The Oil Station will open for business next Wednesday [July 11]," a woman wrote from Sawtelle, near Santa Monica in Los Angeles County in 1928, "and it looks very nice. I went to the City Hall with the Jap to get his License; his name is I. Koga. They will give 2 quarts of Oil with every five gallons of gas for 3 days."

California's automobile clubs were the prime caregivers for drivers. They marked roads, printed maps, checked garages,

Private automobile clubs in northern and southern California began in 1900 to contract with garages and hotels, erect road signs, and generally care for motorists. In 2003, Cheda Chevrolet at Point Reyes Station, Marion County, claims, with Contract 93, to be the oldest AAA garage in the nation. (Photograph by author.)

approved hotels and rated restaurants. For instance, members of the Automobile Club of Southern California knew where to get information. Its monthly circulars, such as the one dated June 15, 1920, informed drivers: "Watch for the club [diamond] signs." They marked approval. "The [65] Hotels and [255] garages listed have contracted to give members prompt, courteous, and efficient service at reasonable rates." Furthermore, the club rated the hostelries and provided their rates, which ranged from $1.50 to $6 a night.

In 1925, San Luis Obispo's Milestone Motel coined the term "motel." At this time Los Angeles had one car for every three people; the national average was one in six. Surprisingly, the two private auto clubs designed and erected highway signs until 1947 on state highways, and as late as 1969 on others.

Of course, the automobile promoted tourism, but it also encouraged conservation. On May 19, 1901, San Jose photographer Andrew P. Hall, and a few other chips off the old redwood block formed the Sempervirens Club (Latin for "Redwood"), raised $32 for lobbying, and in 1902 persuaded the legislature to form the Big Basin Redwood State Park, near Santa Cruz. Lumbermen had logged most of the area, but beauty remained. The state creation of this park "in the heart of the Giant Redwoods," as invitations to visit extolled, became the first time where a government, national or state, purchased private land for public recreation.

This "wonder spot of infinite variety," declared an early brochure, was "easily reached by three hours' auto ride from San Francisco over perfect, smooth, easy-grade State Highways of remarkable scenic splendor." The park's original thirty-eight hundred acres have grown to eighteen thousand, testifying to continuing public popularity. In 1919, the Save the Redwoods League came into being to preserve even more stands of these unique California giants. Preserving old-growth redwoods from rapacious lumber companies requires continued and constant vigilance.

Are automobiles helpful or harmful to wilderness conversation? Due to easy transportation, compared to horse or dusty stagecoach, ordinary Californians came to enjoy the beauties of the land. Some areas, like the Yosemite Valley, have been loved to death. Yet, leaving areas isolated and untrodden does not mean pristine preservation. If something only seems commercially viable, someone will be exploiting the land.

Portals of California's Greatest Play Ground.

In 1917, the new highway that linked San Francisco to the coastal redwood belt presented dual opportunities: Tourists came to worship; loggers came to cut. Between 1917 and 1920, Madison Grant, Henry F. Osborne, and John C. Merriam perfected their Save the Redwoods League to protect the beloved fog-eaters that stood as "Portals of California's Greatest Play Ground."

Mining and clear-cutting are just two activities causing long-lasting ecological damage.

Flying Machines Take Off!

Curious Californians gazed skyward. Since Gold Rush days, hot air balloons were crowd-pleasers. "I went out to the [Baker's Beach] park last Sunday [March 2, 1890]," a San Franciscan remarked, "and saw a man [Thomas Scott Baldwin] go up [1000 feet] in a balloon and come down in a parachute, [which he invented in 1885]. He did not strike quite as soon as he expected and came down in the bay about 300 feet from the shore. He looked like a drowned rat when he came in. There was a big crowd [of 15,000]; most every one that did not go to church. That ain't many. This isn't much of a city for church going."

Southern California, though, witnessed aviation breakthroughs. Near San Diego, on August 28, 1883, John J. Montgomery soared six hundred feet on his twenty-three-foot homemade glider. He developed proper wing shape and flight controls; his observations, published in 1894, became required reading for airplane pioneers Wilbur and Orville Wright. Montgomery's gliders, dropped at four thousand feet from balloons, became familiar carnival sights in the new century, and in 1911 he perished in an airplane crash while in partnership with Victor Loughead (Lockheed).

Early in the twentieth century, Los Angeles became an aviation center. The City of Angels held the nation's first air meet in 1910, a year after Paris hosted the world's first. San Diegan Glenn Curtiss flew his "June Bug" flying machine in 1908 and went on to pioneer naval aviation.

Glenn L. Martin began building mail planes in 1909, while in 1914 Donald Douglas joined him. Six years later, Douglas started his own aircraft company, remarking in 1920 that only

In January 1910, Los Angeles hosted the country's first air show where fifty thousand daily marveled at the "human birds" and California's aerospace industry soared. On November 17, 1918, more than one hundred planes took to the air over San Diego to celebrate the end of World War I.

in California would civilian aircraft manufacturing "first obtain real success." During the 1930s, Californians became more "air-minded," as a woman remarked in 1935, as she watched "the great aluminum sky birds taking form." Gone were the pioneer manufacturing methods using wood, wire, and cloth. During World War II, the 160,000 men and women of Douglas Aircraft Company would build almost 30,000 planes, 16 percent of all produced. In the 1930s, Martin would create the famed Pan American China Clipper mail seaplanes that left from Treasure Island in San Francisco Bay.

Similarly, in 1911, Allan and Malcolm Lockheed began manufacturing seaplanes, and soon John K. Northrop became part of the firm. In the 1920s, T. Claude Ryan inaugurated the first daily flights in the nation by flying between Los Angeles and San Diego, and in 1927 built Charles Lindbergh's trans-Atlantic monoplane, "The Spirit of St. Louis." Another Los Angelean, Harris "Pop" Hanshue began an airline in 1926 that carried 267 passengers. In 1929 his Transcontinental and Western Airlines (transformed into TWA) flew over twenty-five thousand travelers, and became the first air service to make a profit without a government mail contract.

Gushers Galore

Appropriately for new automobile and airplane ages, a Southern California oil boom began in 1898, capitalizing on a promise begun in 1865, when Petrolia, Humboldt County, gave birth to the first producing California well. Emma Summers taught piano in Los Angeles as derricks sprang up around her. She used her eyes to place her money. In 1900, she controlled and brokered fifty thousand barrels a month, half the production of the Los Angeles field.

Lake View #1 erupted spectacularly in March 1910 at Maricopa in the Midway-Sunset Oilfields southwest of Bakersfield. This grand gusher produced 9 million barrels of oil in eighteen months, making Kern County "First in Oil."

Edward Doheny began the Los Angeles oil boom in 1892, but the greatest California oil well of all was Long Beach's Signal Hill, drilled in 1921.

Opportunities came for others on a lesser scale. "I am now starting at Rig building," a husband in Coalinga wrote his San Francisco-based wife in 1903, "and shall receive $3.50 a day and board myself." He promised, "I shall send you money as fast as I am paid," being "sure I can save three dollars a day."

With such success stories at hand, for the next twenty years, the populace acted on the theory that when "drills go down; stocks go up!" Certain Southern California place-names became associated with oil drilling districts: Kern River, Coalinga, Sunset, Midway, McKittrick, Cat Canyon, Arroyo Gande, Elk Hills, Lompoc, Orcutt, Ventura Avenue, Summerland, West Coyote, Montebello, Richfield, Santa Fe Springs, and Signal Hill.

151

A real need of oil for transportation and to power factories drove the oil boom. In 1910, California produced 77 million barrels, and the pace continued to increase. A Kern County oil worker declared in May 1919, "We surely rush things here and every thing is speed. The new well was started last night at midnight and when I left it at three this afternoon it was almost three hundred feet deep and still going."

When a well struck oil, anything could happen. According to a worker, one day, the bit punched through a hard layer into oil sand, "when bang out of the hole came water, mud, stones and gas. On one side of the rig it is ten feet to the ground and the tool dresser fell out of the derrick and lit a running. Mac, the superintendent, fell over the casing pile and crawled on his hands and knees to the engine house. He says he could not have gone any faster on his feet. [The writer, too] beat it into the engine house and stayed there while the well bombarded the surrounding territory with big stones and shale." Following this unusual and unwanted rain, he added, "It is flowing oil now."

Urban Life

Earthquake!

California, north and south, is earthquake country. When tremors hit urban areas, the result is often devastating. At 5:12 A.M. on April 18, 1906, San Francisco experienced a spectacularly violent quake. The San Andreas Fault shifted, releasing energy equal to 8.25 on the Richter scale. Buildings rocked and swayed. In particular, many built on land filled in from the Bay collapsed; the new city hall, a grafter's paradise for thirty-five years, tumbled in ruin. As chimneys crumbled, cooking fires spread, grew, and united. Everything that could go wrong with firefighting did—including the death of the

Standing at Mission Street, looking up 6th Street toward Market, refugees have piled their worldly goods, trunks, bundles, and buggies. Smoke from the fires following the massive 1906 earthquake left San Francisco hazy. These people were the lucky ones. The earthquake, fire, and related events caused an estimated three thousand deaths.

chief and the snapping of water mains. The bravery and determination of firemen could not stop disaster.

Fires burned for three days, destroying twenty-eight thousand buildings encompassed in four square miles, and leaving two hundred thousand people homeless. Wide Van Ness Avenue became a firebreak; eastward old San Francisco became rubble. The city officially counted 674 dead, but contemporary historians, charging a cover-up, have tallied three thousand earthquake-related fatalities.

153

A few days after the great fires of April 18–20, 1906, with lingering smoke clouding the air, a policeman stands at Market and 7th Streets. Behind him is a horse-drawn wagon, the motive power that would rebuild the city, and a flock of sightseers. Government social services were few and fraternal organizations filled the gap. The impressive ruins are those of the Independent Order of Odd Fellows temple.

A trail cleared through the rubble allows a line of commuters to head down Market Street to the Ferry Building and refuge in the East Bay area.

Parks became campgrounds for some 200,000 homeless, over half the city's population. Men talk, children play between rows of white Army tents in Golden Gate Park, and a well-dressed woman keeps her skirt out of the dust. A line of cooking stoves separates the tents.

"Our house is a complete wreck from the Earthquake; the only one on the block that went down," a woman wrote a friend on April 21. It "rocked and shook and then made a final plunge and dropped a sheer 6 feet off the foundation and about 8 feet to one side. The neighbors thought surely we were all killed, but thank God we got out, all of us without a scratch."

In spite of all, she remained positive: "The city is surely in a terrible plight, but all seem to be making the best of it. We are as comfortable as could be expected under the circumstances and are camping in Golden Gate Park with thousands of others like us."

155

The depopulated city gradually returned to normal and rebuilt. In those days of horsepower, thousands of horses worked to their deaths. Literally out of the ashes rose steel-framed concrete buildings, and through the twentieth century, building codes became stricter. The 1915 Panama-Pacific International Exposition honored the rebuilt city and the opening of the Panama Canal. Almost 20 million people visited a jeweled city on San Francisco's Marina. With the memory of that legendary fair in mind, in 1939 and 1940, the Golden Gate International Exposition on manmade Treasure Island rejoiced over the new Bay Bridge (1936) and Golden Gate Bridge (1937).

California's Endless Thirst

The prime requirement for the growth of any area was basic: water. Throughout the twentieth century, population pressure battered this fragile resource. For example, in 1880, Los Angeles had 11,000 residents; in 1890, it had 50,000; in 1900, it had 100,000; in 1905, the total was 200,000; and in 1910, it was 320,000. Growth came without ambience. A young woman arrived from Buffalo, New York, on Christmas Day 1917, and wrote, "First impressions of Los Angeles was how old, how big, how disappointing." Yet, even disappointed people suffered from thirst. In 1902, engineer William Mulholland convinced Los Angeles basin voters to approve the first of many water bonds to finance aqueducts. Beginning in 1908 and culminating in 1913, Los Angeles raided vital water from the Owens Valley, leaving it parched.

However, people continued to require more and more water. In 1920, the city's census recorded 576,000 inhabitants, making it larger than San Francisco. By the mid-1920s, as the City of Angels approached a million inhabitants, Mulholland looked east to the largely untouched Colorado River and lusted after its water. Still Los Angeles grew, an undistinguished city. In 1930, as the city's population soared to 1,238,000, Yugoslav-born Louis Adamic, who wrote pungently on the American immigrant experience, found Los Angeles "colorless, flat, often irksome and depressing."

Los Angeles continued to battle other regions, especially Arizona and Mexico, for water, resulting in a contentious 1929 Colorado River-sharing agreement. In 1927, the legislature authorized regional water districts, and Congress approved Boulder (also known as Hoover) Dam. "We are on a motor trip for a few days," a Californian scribbled on a postcard in 1935, "Visited Boulder Dam, colossal and staggering in construction." Workmen finished this 726.4 foot high Arizona-Nevada dam near Las Vegas, Nevada, that year, while the system of pipes and pumps began Los Angeles delivery in 1941. Los Angeles, though, was not finished. In 1972, Northern California water began flowing south through the California Aqueduct. Still the insatiable quest continues. A proposed Peripheral Canal to drain even more water from the north is discussed regularly, while Colorado River allocation is continually in the news.

San Francisco, similarly, had to resolve a water crisis, and in addition, it had to buy out the private Spring Valley Water Company. In 1901, city officials planned to bring in 400 million gallons daily by gravity flow to serve 4 million Bay Area people. The water would come from damming Hetch Hetchy, the "Grand Canyon of the Tuolumne," in Yosemite National Park. "I never handled any proposition where the engineering problems were so simple and the political ones so complex," hydraulic engineer Michael Maurice O'Shaughnessy declared. His most vocal foes were "alleged nature lovers"—the "tree-huggers" of today— John Muir and the Sierra Club, who did not wish to see one of the most beautiful valleys of California disappear.

From 1901 to 1969, Angel's Flight, the "World's Shortest Railroad" carried passengers from downtown Third Street Los Angeles to upper-class housing on the top of Bunker Hill. Five cents bought a ride on two counterbalanced cars, Sinai and Olivet. "NOTICE: $50 fine for riding or driving through this tunnel faster than a walk," reads the 1907-era sign. Following redevelopment of Bunker Hill, Angel's Flight reopened in 1996 a half-block further down Hill Street. (Photograph by Warren C. Dickerson.)

However, Congress cleared the way on December 7, 1913, perhaps another "Day of Infamy," and O'Shaughnessy telegraphed home, "Victory at Midnight. San Francisco knows how"—appropriating President William Howard Taft's catchy phrase about the city's spirit. He came to be known to taxpayers as "More Money" O'Shaughnessy, and in 1934 San Francisco received pure Sierra water. In addition, hydroelectric power ran the multitude of electric appliances that came into vogue in the 1920s.

LABOR AND MONEY

Branch Banks and Checking Accounts

The way people handled money changed dramatically in the early twentieth-century. Until the Federal Reserve established in 1918 a nationwide check-clearing system that would pay checks at a distance, few people bothered with bank accounts. Their checks were no good outside their resident town. When paying at a distance most people sent cash by Wells, Fargo & Co.'s Express, or through a postal or express money order. By 1918, Wells Fargo had nine hundred offices within California on all the major railroad, stage, and steamboat lines.

Within cities, bank clearinghouses cashed all local checks, and as populations grew, people began to demand greater financial convenience. In 1908, the Peoples' Water Company in Oakland advised customers, "There are three ways to pay your bill for water: To the Collector, by check, or at the office." It placed emphasis on the second method. Conveniently, customers could have Uncle Sam's mailmen do the walking rather than keeping cash on hand for the former, or making a special trip to the latter.

The Financial Panic of 1907, which began in New York and spread westward, shook up peoples' financial complacency. City banks in San Francisco and Los Angeles banded together to increase the money supply on their own responsibility. They pooled assets to back the Clearing House Certificates they issued. As the supply of U.S. money increased, the banks retired their certificates.

In addition, state banks, laxly controlled, failed while national banks, sternly examined, did not. In 1909, the legislature passed a bank law that overhauled the state regulatory system established in 1879. It permitted departmental banking; that is, one bank could offer commercial, savings, and trust services rather than having to maintain separate institutions. The law also allowed branch banking, which had fallen out of favor since the Gold Rush.

Branch banking was nothing new to Californians. Adams & Co. and Wells, Fargo & Co. had bank branches in the early 1850s, while the Bank of California and Wells Fargo had interstate bank offices through the nineteenth century. However, it took a retired agricultural produce buyer who knew the state intimately to understand the advantages of retail branch banking. Beginning with the Bank of Italy in 1904, through the 1920s, Amadeo Peter Giannini fought regulators with as much fervor as he fought the competition to establish a statewide branch banking system thirty years ahead of any competitor. Transformed into the Bank of America in 1930, in 1945 it was the world's largest financial organization.

Labor Unions Battle the Open Shop

That rolling ocean, the great Pacific, nourished San Francisco commerce. However, the San Francisco waterfront was never tame; work was hard, hours long, and rights few. Shanghaiing,

In November 1907, a New York City financial panic spread west. Without a Federal Reserve System, which began in 1913, banks throughout the nation joined in their clearing house associations. They put up securities and issued emergency money. Clearing House certificates, in denominations of $1, $2, $5, $10, and $20 expanded the money supply for three months.

or kidnapping men, mostly Scandinavian immigrants, for crews, was common into the twentieth century. Employers ruled, temporarily hiring sailors and the longshoremen who unloaded cargoes through biased labor contractors, who played favorites and accepted bribes.

Longshoremen and teamsters, who hauled goods from the docks to warehouses (the current logo of the Teamsters' Union has two horse heads), fought back with their only weapon, organization, often backed with violence against strike-breakers. During the harvest season from July 30 to October 2, 1901, these oppressed workingmen halted waterfront activity. When the strike ended, all accepted the right of unions to exist, and San Francisco became the most unionized city on the Pacific.

The history of labor in Southern California was different altogether. In Los Angeles, Harrison Gray Otis, publisher of the Los Angeles *Times*, led the charge for an open shop, that is, one that hired lower-paid non-union members. Otis claimed that only cheap labor costs would allow the City of Angels to compete against San Francisco and eastern manufacturers. Wages remained up to 40 percent lower than in the Bay City across all industries. In May 1910, several unions went on strike, the city passed an anti-picketing ordinance, and on October 1, disaster struck. A bomb exploded in the *Times* building, killing twenty and wounding seventeen. After labor leaders John and James McNamara confessed to setting the device, the labor movement collapsed.

The same violent tactics brought labor leaders similarly counterproductive results in San Francisco. There, the issue of handling non-union produced goods still festered, and it erupted in a strike by the Riggers and Stevedores' Union from June 1 to July 20, 1916. On June 22, the Chamber of Commerce came out for open-shop hiring, and on July 10, it formed a Law and Order Committee, a tradition harking back to the Committee of Vigilance of 1851, to stamp out "lawlessness." As the water-front returned somewhat to normal on July 20, labor protested increasing American involvement in the First World War.

The Chamber saw the United States being sucked into World War I and on July 22, 1916, they sponsored a Prepared-ness Day Parade for what it saw as America's eventual entry. Suddenly, in the midst of revelers, a suitcase bomb studded with nails and bullets exploded at Market and Steuart Streets, killing ten and wounding forty. A mass meeting denounced the act, and soon the Law and Order Committee had $1 million pledged. Using the Progressives' program of the initiative, on November 7, business owners convinced voters to "prohibit picketing." Officials never caught the perpetrators, assumed to have been labor unionists. They instead framed radical labor leader Tom Mooney, an iron molder. International protest against such social injustice finally won Mooney a pardon on January 7, 1939.

The year 1919 was a bad one for radicals and labor unions. While the U.S. Attorney General trumpeted a "Red Scare," warning against the godless Communist Russian Bolsheviks, California passed a criminal syndicalism law, which provided for the arrest of anyone accepting or using violence to bring social change. It remained enforced until 1968. Another long-shoremen's strike erupted on September 15, 1919, resulting in the collapse of the Riggers and Stevedores' Union. An employer-run union emerged, controlling San Francisco waterfront hiring until 1934. Each port of the Pacific Coast had specific rules, but loose groups of shippers dominated employment at all of the harbors. The Great Depression, that national economic collapse which began in 1929 and lasted through the 1930s, brought orga-nized labor to the docks.

Seaport Strike Leads to Organized Labor

President Franklin D. Roosevelt fought the Great Depression on many fronts. The New Deal's National Recovery Act of June 16, 1933, contained the famed Section 7a: "Employees shall have the right to organize and bargain collectively, through representatives of their own choosing." By the end of the year, it had killed the employers' waterfront labor union.

In September 1933, the International Longshoremen's Association (ILA), gone from the waterfront since 1919, returned, determined to bring unity and dignity to longshoremen. In 1934, radical leaders took over the union, the foremost being Australian-born, thirty-three-year-old Harry Bridges, a San Francisco stevedore since 1922. Bridges has since been deified in San Francisco with his own Plaza by the Ferry Building (1999), and "Bridges Day" on July 28, 2001. Bridges combined knowledge of the situation with eloquence and charisma, but in the next strike, workers' militancy outran their leaders.

On May 9, 1934, radicals shut down Seattle, Tacoma, Portland, San Francisco, and San Pedro (Los Angeles) ports. In the Bay City, unionists attacked strikebreakers and African Americans, who kept working since the union kept them out (a ban Bridges would reverse). May 12 saw five hundred strikers attack the employers' headquarters, and the next day, the teamsters refused to haul goods to and from the docks.

With absolute correctness, the ILA chortled, "With the Teamsters behind us, we've got them licked," and the strike spread to other maritime unions. As employers moved goods on the Belt Line Railroad, strikers adopted the tactics of Mahatma Gandhi of India, blocking the tracks with their autos and their bodies. On May 15, 1934, not one freighter left San Francisco, while in Los Angeles, the employer stronghold of the Pacific Coast, three hundred strikers attacked a stockade holding "scab" labor, with one man killed.

Through the rest of May, rioting increased, more maritime unions joined the strikers, and all repudiated efforts of mediators Joseph P. Ryan, president of the International Longshoremen's Association, and Assistant Secretary of Labor Edward F. McGrady. As Bridges came to the fore, McGrady denounced the "red element," which "lives on strikes and does not want settlement."

Positions hardened in June. When the Industrial Association, a businessmen's anti-union group (formed in 1921), called for "Opening the Port," the Teamsters on June 7 flatly refused to haul any more goods. While shippers had seventeen hundred strikebreakers loading and unloading, they could not get merchandise to the docks. On June 16, both sides signed an agreement. Although the teamsters went back to work, the rank and file of the maritime unions promptly repudiated the deal and their leaders.

Ten unions then formed the Marine Strike Committee, placed six thousand men at the ready, increased violence, and looked "Forward to a General Strike." On June 27, ILA President Ryan—not the Chamber of Commerce—declared, "Bridges doesn't want this strike settled and it is my firm belief he is acting for the Communists."

Meantime, the Industrial Association formed the Atlas Trucking Company, with at most forty trucks, to carry merchandise from Pier 38, at the foot of Townsend Street, to a King Street warehouse, both near the current Pacific Bell Park. The non-union truckers, guarded by a strong police escort, began work on July 3, 1934.

The crisis came following Independence Day. On July 5, the so-called Bloody Thursday, five thousand strikers battled first the trucks then the Belt Railway. Two strikers, longshoreman Howard Sperry and cook and Communist Nicholas Counderakis (or Bordois), died on Mission Street, near the union headquarters in the still-standing Audiffred Building. One hundred and nine strikers were injured when police attacked entrenched unionists in the Battle of Rincon Hill.

Governor Frank F. Merriam, citing Communist influence, called out the National Guard, and a force of fifteen hundred secured the waterfront. The Joint Marine Strike Committee, for its part, declared, "The San Francisco Industrial Association and the San Francisco Police have started a reign of terror on the waterfront by shooting, gassing and bombing the workers." It demanded a general strike.

"In all my thirty years of leading these men I have never seen them so worked up, so determined to walk out," Teamsters president Michael Casey pronounced. Trying for calmness, Casey said, "The Teamsters here have absolutely no grievance of their own to settle." On July 8, 1934, a Teamsters vote of 1,220 to 271 repudiated Casey and moderation, and united them with their more radical brethren. On the next day, the unions buried their two martyrs. Thousands of strikers, with no police present, formed an orderly, solemn, and silent line stretching a mile-and-a-half down Market Street. The workers of San Francisco turned out to pay tribute.

On July 12, 1934, the formerly conservative Teamsters joined dockworkers, walked out, and surprised the city. They established a blockade south across the peninsula and at the ferry landings; on July 16, 115 unions, some 50,000 men, joined the general strike. San Francisco shut down. The mayor quickly assumed emergency powers and increased troops to six thousand. The next day, unknown citizens, said to have been conservative laboring men, mobbed and destroyed various Communist headquarters. The police arrived immediately afterwards, arresting 270.

With food and gasoline scarce, popular support quickly deserted the strikers. On July 18, within three hours ten thousand people signed a petition calling for martial law, and the strike collapsed after seventy-seven hours. On July 20, the Teamsters, the crucial element, voted 1,138 to 283 to return to work.

By July 27, 1934, the crisis had passed and the troops left. Longshoremen and seamen in San Francisco accepted arbitration by the National Longshoremen's Board 2,014 to 722, and 4,305 to 409. That board settled Pacific Coast issues, giving the unions most of their demands. A day's work became six hours. Straight time rose 10 cents to 95 cents an hour, while overtime jumped from $1.25 to $1.40 an hour. Best of all, unions now had a joint voice in the operation of hiring halls. With control of hiring halls secured, membership in the ILA ballooned eight times, and by 1937 stood at fifty thousand.

THE GREAT DEPRESSION AND ITS REMEDIES

The stock market crash in October 1929 ushered in the Great Depression, which, in the early thirties brought nationwide economic collapse, hundreds of bank failures, and one-third unemployment. By June 1934, the lusterless Golden State saw seven hundred thousand workers unemployed, half in Los Angeles County, out of a 1930 state population of 5.7 million. A fifth of that county received relief—a meager $16.20 per family per month; common labor had long been a dollar a day.

While constant labor strife hit all the major farming areas and seaports, other areas of the nation were worse off in the Depression years. Their migrants became California's problem. Huge dust storms (particularly in Oklahoma) stripped off fertile topsoil and forced southwestern farmers from their land. They headed west. These were the despised "Okies," the supposed "poor white trash," who made Bakersfield a center of country and western music. A sensitive John Steinbeck graphically told of the nomads' plight in his famous *The Grapes of Wrath* (1939), honored in 2002 as the novel all Californians should read.

With Southern California hit especially hard by the depression, a plan for salvation came in 1934 from Pasadenan Upton Sinclair. This Christian socialist had exposed the horrible conditions of Chicago meat-packing plants in his book *The Jungle* (1906) and Southern California corruption in his book *Oil!* (1927), recently reprinted as a California classic. In 1934 he became the Democratic candidate for governor.

Socialist Sinclair's plan to "End Poverty in California" (EPIC) proposed to have the state seize idle farmland and factories for the benefit of cooperatives, which would exchange products for scrip, not backed up with any assets. Furthermore, those over sixty years of age would receive a $50 a month pension. To pay for this, Sinclair proposed to repeal the sales tax, which disproportionately fell on the poor, and instead institute an income tax and increase levies on corporations. Preceding the election, one thousand EPIC Clubs spread over the state, primarily in Southern California.

Shocked Republicans charged that "Communist" Sinclair would "Russianize California." His plan to "(E)nd (P)roperty; (I)ntroduce (C)ommunism," opponents declared, would lead to "Easy Pickings In California." As proof, Hollywood fabricated newsreels showing hordes of "Bums and Bolsheviks" pouring into the Golden State—images, incidentally, confirming California's bounty and status as a favored destination for those seeking a land of promise.

One disgruntled conservative wrote from San Pedro on March 16, 1936, "If the present situation continues, I am tempted to move to Canada and get away from this mess of taxes and alphabets, the EPICs and Utopians and Townsenders and all the rest."

LET'S GO TO THE MOVIES

Californians escaped the reality of the Depression by focusing on Clark Gable and Mae West at the movies. In 1902, Los Angeles opened the nation's first movie theater, and producers D.W. Griffith, Cecil B. DeMille, Jesse Lasky, Samuel Goldwyn, David Belasco, and Mack Sennett creatively forged the new medium of silent movies. Hollywood in the south and Niles, near Oakland in the north, became production centers, while Wells, Fargo & Co.'s Express service rushed new releases to theaters throughout the nation.

Movie palaces caught the popular imagination. In 1915, Clunes Auditorium Theatre at Fifth and Olive Streets in Los Angeles, advertised itself as the "Largest Motion Picture Theatre in America. Seats 3000. $30,000 Pipe Organ. 25 Piece Orchestra. Largest Theatre Electric Sign in the World—Six stories above the roof."

In 1927, Grauman's Chinese Theatre, a lavish Los Angeles landmark, opened with a showing of Cecil B. DeMille's epic *The King of Kings*. Still splendid, handprints of stars adorn its front sidewalk. With audiences unable to hear what stars actually said—subtitles performed that function—silent movies emphasized gesture, facial expression, and body movement. The movie musical *Singin' in the Rain* (Metro-Goldwyn-Mayer, 1952) starring Gene Kelly and Debbie Reynolds, captures the spirit of this era. Audiences thrilled to Clara Bow, James Cagney, Charlie Chaplin, Douglas Fairbanks, Greta Garbo, Jean Harlow, Tom Mix, Mary Pickford, and Rudolph Valentino.

"Talkies" began with the sweet sounds of Al Jolson, filmed in San Francisco in *The Jazz Singer* (Warner Brothers, 1927). The silent films vanished, actors had to develop additional talents, and production costs soared. Color came in 1935, adding

169

Stars on the Hollywood Walk of Fame, Los Angeles.

more processes and cost for motion picture production, and Bank of America was in the forefront making loans to the new industry. Animator Walt Disney enlivened the dull Depression 1930s with a soon world-famous optimistic cartoon mouse and an ill-tempered duck. Millions of children grew up wishing to meet Mickey Mouse and Donald Duck, and beginning in 1955 they could, with the opening of Disneyland in Anaheim.

A Southern California college fraternity boy wrote in his diary in 1916, "With my Honey all day." They "went to picture show. Saw the 'Devil's Daughter.' Very good." Ten years later, the State Theater in Martinez offered "popular pictures at popular prices," 10 and 30 cents. Included was a staged performance featuring singing, dancing, and slapstick comedy featured as "A Gigantic Vaudeville Show Every Sunday." Thrown in were "lessons in Charleston," the latest unrestrained dance craze, so that young men and women could emulate popular artist Thomas Held Jr.'s sheiks and flappers. A prime requisite for a chic sheik was an automobile. Women dressed to make themselves look as slender as possible, bobbed their hair short, wore short skirts, smoked, and, even though this was during Prohibition, drank alcohol. An added State Theater bonus, enlivened with peculiar spelling, was "Community Singing with Song Cartunes." The audience followed the words with a "bouncing ball" acting as a pointer.

Among the State's 1926 silent films, which it changed every two days, were *The Road to Mandalay*, *The Belle of Broadway*, and *Her Honor the Governor*. Other popular movies included thrillers, such as *The Flying Mail*, *The Lone Wolf Returns*, and *The Runaway Express*. The exuberant *Son of the Sheik* starred heartthrob Rudolph Valentino and Vilma Ranky, "with eyes more fiery, lips more magnetic, and romance more electric," all at "no advance in prices." Soon came *Some Pun'kins*, advertised as "a homespun story without Sheiks or Sex."

171

Today, fanatic fans follow favorite movie stars, grasping the latest gossip of affairs or non-affairs, gobbling down with their eyes the latest releases, taking tours of movie mansions, and congregating at the intersection of Hollywood and Vine. Hollywood's star-studded Walk of Fame stretches along Hollywood Boulevard between Gower Street and La Brea Avenue, and on the Vine Street axis from Yucca Street to Sunset Boulevard. Here Governor Arnold Schwarzenegger has embedded star status. To the world, regardless of their resemblance to real life, Hollywood's productions are America writ large.

INNOCENCE IN A TIME OF TURMOIL

Time often lends a soft romance to the past, but the first forty years of the twentieth century were not kind to California. No era really is calm and uneventful to those living through it. In spite of earthquakes, economic stagnation, ethnic and immigration turmoil, urban ills, labor strife, radical politics, and the Great War, Californians retained a love of life.

College opportunities of all descriptions expanded; in 1910, the first public junior college in the nation opened in Fresno. This chapter begins with a young boy becoming a teenager; college students will close it.

In 1916, a Southern California student wrote in his diary, "Went to church and chapel; played more cards." Dorm monitors were active: "Got stung for smoking;" and "Had booz party in my room." None of this, of course, would happen today. . . .

Ten years later came a carefree Stanford University coed. In 1937, she went light-heartedly to a disciplinary review either, as she phrased it, for "one of the eight parking tickets [a goodly number!], or for signing out [from the dorms] too many times (on purpose—I couldn't miss seeing "Captains Courageous.)"

Meantime, a Stanford friend made basketball history. Future Hall-of-Famer Hank Luisetti developed the one-handed shot. At Madison Square Garden, New York City, on December 30, 1936, Luisetti's prowess ended Long Island University's forty-six-game winning streak. "Won all the way," the Stanford team captain telegraphed about this 45–31 victory. "Guess they can beat anyone now!" his girlfriend responded. "In the East they play more conservatively," Stanford coach John Bunn, also honored in the Hall of Fame, remarked to the press. "They shoot with two hands, with both feet on the floor. We take the chances."

The team's reward? "One boy sends all his best to one girl asking for one date" the captain telegraphed from St. Paul. "If answer is No, prepare for indefinite merciless siege on [the residence hall] doorstep. Hank is included in date, so make it two. Please. California, here we come." The result: "Date granted, but the boys got snowbound on the train and stood us up— almost. Hot Choc at the Creamery and their charming selves seemed pretty good to us."

Within four years such innocence would vanish as a grim war worldwide would engulf the nation and California's Pacific Coast location would play a pivotal role. Even the annoyance of snow-bound railroads would disappear as Americans took to the air. Time does not stand still, and the remainder of the twentieth century would hurry the pace of change.

AIR CORPS
TRAINING DETACHMENT
KING CITY, CALIF.

A King City Army Air Corps Training Center decal in muted yellow, orange, and green exhibits a flat, art deco style of Southwest painting made famous by Maynard Dixon. In the south, Marines trained at Camp Pendleton (Rancho Santa Margarita), while General George S. Patton's tanks rumbled across deserts resembling North Africa.

CHAPTER V

Trendsetter for a Nation

(1940–2003)

"Sunday morning, December 7, we went out on the beach [at Lanikai] before breakfast to see the airplanes," my aunt wrote from Hawaii in 1941. "There were about one hundred and were flying very high. They were so pretty in the sun, just like silver." Explosions on that "Day of Infamy" shattered the idyllic moment. "We could see the big rising sun on the wings," she wrote. "We were [scared]; everybody was scared. It was so sudden and so terrible." And so the Second World War came to United States soil.

California's industrial and agricultural might became crucial to the war effort, especially in the Pacific. Men went off to war; women went into the workforce; civilians coped with rationing and restriction; and unity and cooperation prevailed. Industry, now almost tripling in size, needed a new labor force once more. This time, black men and women came from the Southeast. They filled the void left by another labor force—as 110,000 Japanese Americans were confined to War Relocation Camps. Postwar California became even more complex, with a multiethnic, greatly urban population numbering 35 million. Although economic, cultural, social, and environmental concerns change rapidly, California remains the place to be.

WAR!

War brought the usual, wrenching separations to Californians. On December 14, 1942, a year and a week after the war began, a lovesick sailor in San Diego declared to his "Little Twinkle Eyes" in Los Angeles that, "We sure did have a wonderful time dancing to the records of ours. It sure would be swell to hold you in my arms and go dancing around the room." A wife asked in 1943, "Oh, gee, Honey. Please make the war get over quick so that I can have you all to my selfish self again, won't you huh?"

That same year, inflammatory headlines from William Randolph Hearst's Los Angeles *Examiner* showed a grimmer side of war. Heir to a vast fortune made in mining, Hearst took control in 1887 of the San Francisco *Examiner*, which became the foundation for a nationwide string of nationalistic, opinionated dailies. His Southern California paper began in 1903. Today, this powerful, journalistic genius is best known through Orson Welles' movie "Citizen Kane" (1941) and from his lavish castle at San Simeon, now a state park. This sampling emphasizes two of the paper's main themes: rationing and racism.

"The Office of Price Administration tonight reduced A, B and C gasoline ration coupon values in the Far West from four to three gallons, each, effective at midnight." (October 12, 1943)

"Hundreds of Thousands [in China] Slaughtered in New Wave of Bestial Jap Atrocities." (October 31, 1943)

"WARREN WARNS OF NIP PERIL—Presence of many thousand Japanese in California including 'so many of those admittedly American-hating Japs' in the Tule Lake Relocation Center constitutes a 'positive danger to the state, and a threat to the war effort,'

Governor [Earl] Warren told a press conference today."
(November 6, 1943)

"Beans and Peas to Rule 1944 California Menus." [So
many fighting men ate up local supplies passing
through California to embark for the war in the Pacific
that] "Californians apt to get less meat and fish than
the national average." (November 6, 1943)

"Additional troops and armored equipment were
reported ordered into the strike-bound Tule Lake seg-
regation camp today as sullen Japanese remained
defiant and the situation continued tense. This move, it
was said, was ordered as a 'protective measure' against
further outbreaks among the 16,000 admittedly disloyal
internees." (November 15, 1943)

"Unguarded Jap Internees Fish and Picnic at L.A. Water
Source" [at Poston, Arizona.] (November 18, 1943)

"JAPS HIDE KNIVES, FOOD IN ARIZONA INTERNMENT
CAMP. Japanese interned in the Rivers camp, in the
war-vital Phoenix Valley in Arizona, have staged
strikes, stolen knives and other weapons, cached lavishly supplied food and wasted supplies in flagrant
contempt for the War Relocation Authority's officials."
(November 22, 1943)

INCARCERATION OF JAPANESE AMERICANS

These last headlines spoke to a product of war common to
most of the world, but rare to the American experience: people
driven away from their homes as refugees and imprisoned in

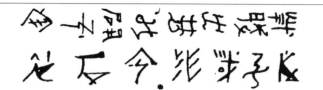

SOUTHERN CALIFORNIANS ATTENTION!

Suppose these were Jap bombers overhead . . . the spearhead of an invasion force!

Suppose this was a Jap proclamation calling on us to surrender or suffer the fate of Hongkong or Singapore!

THIS COULD HAPPEN HERE!

And it WILL . . . unless we give our fighting men the planes, tanks and guns they must have to make Victory certain.

Your support is urgently needed today in the 2nd War Loan Drive to raise 13 billion fighting dollars during April. Remember—you are asked not to give, but to INVEST in the world's finest security — United States Government Bonds.

Go to any bank, post office, savings and loan association, store or theatre where War Bonds are sold and buy at least one EXTRA Bond this week. There is an investment for every purse from $18.75 to $1,000,000. Do your part for Victory.

They Give Their Lives—You Lend Your Dollars

"This Could Happen Here!" declared an April 1943 southern California war bond drive notice warning of an Imperial Japanese invasion. At this time, local Japanese-American neighbors had been swept into relocation camps. Ignorance placed imaginary Japanese writing sideways in the mock surrender demand, but the appeal to American patriotism raised $18.5 billion nationally, $5.5 billion over this drive's goal.

relocation camps. Exceptions in U.S. history include Southern refugees of the Civil War and Native Americans confined to reservations.

When the United States went to war in December 1941, few were confident that it would win; nor did anyone underestimate the fighting prowess of the imperial Japanese forces. Fear united with a long history of anti-Japanese sentiment. As far back as June 1919, Democratic Senator James D. Phelan pronounced that "unquestionable evidence" showed that the Japanese had "a racial loathing for the people of the United States." Significantly, he added, "In case of a conflict with Japan, we would have to meet, not only a frontal attack, but a rear attack." At the beginning of hostilities, anti-Japanese feeling found an outlet against 110,000 residents of California. This 1 percent of the population would be removed and confined to refugee camps.

The shocking injustice of this act is clear today. Japanese Americans, with their strong sense of culture and morality, committed no overt acts against their host nation, and the Japanese in Hawaii, who formed over a third of the population, were not evacuated. Furthermore, thirty-three thousand Japanese Americans served in the armed forces during the war. Infantry units, such as the 442nd Regimental Combat Team, fought valiantly through the European Theater. The "Go For Broke," with 18,143 medals, became the most highly decorated unit in American history, demonstrating incredible bravery and casualties. Of course, Japanese American patriotism during World War II is no assurance that another group of immigrants would be so law-abiding during another war—but their record is cautionary, as the United States conducts a "war on terror."

On February 19, 1942, two and a half months after Pearl Harbor, as the Japanese won victory after victory in the

Pacific, President Franklin Delano Roosevelt signed Executive Order 9066. Roosevelt argued under the 1860s Civil War guise of "military necessity," that in order to protect "against espionage and against sabotage to national-defense materials, national-defense premises, and national-defense utilities," he would authorize the Secretary of War to "prescribe military areas" from "which any or all persons may be excluded." Congress concurred on March 21.

Specifically, this meant that the War Relocation Authority would prevent any of the 127,000 Japanese in the country from living in eight western states. On May 7, 1942, 107,000 Japanese began to move to assembly centers, and on June 5, into ten camps around the nation. The rapid uprooting caused internees to lose personal possessions, farms, and businesses. Currently, Japanese Americans mark February 19 as a "Day of Remembrance."

The Federal government did not imprison Japanese in their home states. Out-of-staters came to California's two camps, Manzanar (Spanish for "apple orchard") and Tule Lake. Manzanar, the oldest, began on March 23, 1942, in the remote Owens Valley. It housed nine thousand internees by the fall of 1942, employing four thousand in the camp and another one thousand harvesting sugar beets in Montana and Idaho. Eager hands rehabilitated six hundred apple and four hundred pear trees, to harvest a crop worth $2,000. Many now know of the camp from Ansel Adams' photographs taken to protest Japanese American incarceration. In 1992, Manzanar became a National Historic Site, and the Park Service is presently restoring the administration building and a mess hall. Tule Lake, which confined the most rebellious inmates, sat in the far northeast near Oregon. By fall 1942, its Japanese Americans had harvested thirteen hundred tons of potatoes and vegetables from a twenty-six hundred acre farm at the site.

The WRA made the best of a bad job, and many of its members were merciful within the confines of their orders. Government reports and circulars contain none of the bitterness and hatred of the *Examiner*, and officials attempted to keep families and communities together. For instance, San Franciscans went to central Utah near Delta, Imperial Valley Japanese Americans traveled to the Colorado River Relocation Center, and residents of Tulare and Turlock found themselves on the Gila River.

In the camps, authorities mandated self-government, newspapers, schools, postal services, entrepreneurial retail shops, and recreation. They provided paid employment within the camps, and allowed leaves for harvest labor. By September 1942, those not suspected of disloyalty could leave the camps if they could find jobs elsewhere.

The camps themselves certainly were unpleasant and oppressive. The wartime shortage of building materials continually hampered efforts to keep inmates warm and healthy. Furthermore, cramped, crowded conditions disrupted family structure and authority. The WRA report for the quarter ending September 30, 1942, recognized the strife between the Issei (born in Japan), who reacted with "passive non-resistance" and the angry Nisei, "conscious of their American citizenship," who became "disillusioned—bitter" at this treatment from their government. Authorities also acknowledged that "the evacuees found a dominant tone of hostility and condemnation directed toward them" from civil society in general.

Yet, Community Analysis Report No. 1, issued in October 1942, encouraged WRA workers to display "a friendly attitude" towards internees. This series of reports, which the War Relocation Authority produced irregularly, inculcated relative cultural sensitivity. For instance, "Sitdowns, strikes and riots are not the result of cussedness," the first report stated, "but are the results of misunderstandings and dissatisfactions." WRA publications, at least, seemed genuinely concerned with causes of internal friction in the camps and worked to alleviate them.

However, Japanese residents of the Pacific Coast would have much preferred their liberty, property, and possessions. In 1942 Minoru Yasui of Oregon, Washingtonian Gordon Hirabayashi, and Fred T. Korematsu of San Leandro, California, fought for their constitutional rights through the courts. They attacked the legal foundation for the orders telling them to leave. Hirabayashi refused to report for relocation, and additionally argued that as an American citizen, a military-instituted curfew demanding he remain inside between 8 P.M. and 6 A.M. was as unjust as it was unconstitutional. His suit became the test case.

In June 1943, the Supreme Court's use of "military necessity" in Hirabayashi's suit to justify detention and its regulations made some members of the court uneasy. Dissenting Justice William O. Douglas stated, "Detention for reasonable cause is one thing. Detention on account of ancestry is another." Dissenting in the similarly resolved Korematsu case on December 18, 1944, Justice Owen J. Roberts found the facts "exhibit a clear violation of Constitutional rights," while Justice Frank Murphy stated, "Such exclusion [from the Pacific Coast] goes over 'the brink of constitutional power,' and falls into the ugly abyss of racism."

That same day in December 1944, on a request for a writ of habeas corpus, the court declared that Mitsuye Endo of Sacramento could go where she wished without following WRA leave procedures. Justice Murphy said, "If, as I believe, the military orders excluding her from California were invalid at the time they were issued, they are increasingly objectionable at this late date." Anticipating the decision, on the previous day the government had allowed Japanese Americans to travel and settle where they wished, and began closing the camps.

Redress came slowly in the postwar period. In 1948, the California Supreme Court became the first in the nation to annul laws prohibiting interracial marriage. On a personal level on December 7, 1958, two movements, labor and civil rights, came together on the anniversary of the Pearl Harbor attack. Noriko Sawada, whose internment fired a passion for civil rights, married Harry Bridges, leader of the International Longshore and Warehouse Union in Nevada, to challenge that state's miscegenation law. However, not until November 10, 1983, did the Ninth Circuit Court of Appeals overturn Korematsu's conviction (reversing its own decision of December 2, 1943), and on September 24, 1987, the same court brought justice to Gordon Hirabayashi.

Appropriately, on August 10, 1988, a Californian, President Ronald Reagan, signed a congressional apology, which also appropriated $20,000 in reparations for each of the sixty-five thousand living internees. This act was sponsored by congressmen Norman Mineta of San Jose and Robert Matsui of Sacramento, who had been children in the camps. With the reparations, the President closed what he called "A sad chapter in American history." At Manzanar a state historical marker reads, "May the injustices and humiliation suffered here as a result of hysteria, racism, and economic exploitation never emerge again."

Former American soldiers carried out their own campaigns for redress, even to former enemies. Some have returned captured swords, some several hundred years old. While serving in the Philippines during the war, a Wells Fargo colleague of mine randomly picked up scattered Japanese correspondence for souvenirs. Fifty years later, he found relatives of the letter-writers. For the grateful families, these scraps became the only remembrances of lost sons. They were astonished at the generosity of a former enemy.

After the war, Japanese Americans for the most part assimilated into mainstream American society. In the 1930s, forty-seven "Japantowns" clustered on the West Coast. Now three remain, in San Francisco, San Jose, and Los Angeles. As one San Jose merchant remarked in 2001, "Since the war, everyone became 200 percent American, so everyone is shopping at Macy's." Furthermore, Japanese-American children did not wish to run labor-intensive traditional family businesses that require long hours. In 1976 Californians sent Samuel Ichiye Hayakawa, who had been an English professor in Illinois during the war, to the U.S. Senate.

Ironically, the internment camps provided another immigrant group with economic opportunity. When the Japanese Americans left, Indians from the state of Gujarat took over many Japanese-run San Francisco hotels, and they now own 38 percent of the nation's hostelries.

Somewhere in the Pacific

Meantime, the war went on, and Californians kept in touch with loved ones through letters. A 1943 wife asked her husband, "How do you like the army and does your uniform fit?" With hard fighting and heavy casualties deleted from censored letters, relatives at home often had to guess at the soldiers' experiences. What soldiers could say was often out of the ordinary. One soldier, stationed "somewhere in the Pacific" (actually the Solomon Islands), wrote on September 12, 1944, about fighting hookworm and amebic dysentery through jelly-bean sized pills and shots that threatened to "finish me off."

The armed forces strictly monitored entertainment as well. "We haven't been seeing very good shows over here, either," the same soldier wrote. "The majority of them are [Technicolor] musicals. I don't mind seeing a good musical once in a while, but right now, I'm tired of musicals." In addition to such lightweight shows, "They showed us some war films presented by the U.S. and British governments last night." The films showed Allied victories: "the final and complete annihilation of the Nazis in Tunisia." The governmental message was plain: "It showed how the land, sea, and air forces were all coordinated to defeat the Germans."

Soldiers also read cheaply printed paperback Armed Services Editions of "the best books of the present and the past," which the Council on Books in Wartime supplied.

Some were lucky enough to see English-born Bob Hope, a Californian by adoption. From his first show at March Air Force Base at Riverside on May 6, 1941, to the last in Saudi Arabia in 1990 during the first Persian Gulf War, Hope's one-liners and pretty girls showed "my kids," as Hope affectionately called the troops, "what they were fighting for." Hope quipped, "We represented everything those new recruits did not have: home cooking, mother, and soft roommates," He added, "The enemies were boredom, mud, officers, and abstinence. Any joke that touched those nerves was a sure thing."

In 1948, when Soviet forces blocked all roads leading into Berlin, Hope began his Christmas shows during the Berlin Air Lift when the Allies brought in all needed supplies by airplane. These shows continued for thirty-four years, allowing Hope to rack up 10 million airline miles entertaining the Armed Forces. In March 1997, the Navy launched the 949-foot USNS *Bob Hope*, the first of a class of ships of that name, capable of carrying all equipment needed for an Army task force. A month later, McDonell Douglas Corporation (now part of Boeing) produced a huge California-built C-17 cargo plane that the Air Force christened "The Spirit of Bob Hope," recalling the spirit that developed fifty years before, out of the dark days of World War II.

One sweltering soldier wrote on May 9, 1945, from Papua, New Guinea, about being drained from "this continuous heat," and wet from the start of the rainy season. "I'll have to do a little fixing up on this tent to keep the rain from flowing in so much. This rain makes good sleeping anyhow." At least, though, he felt, "things here are picking up a little now. We've had fresh meat twice in three days now. Boy was that good, even if it was hamburger." One item worthy of special note was "fresh onions most all the time."

Eventually, American and Allied soldiers achieved victory in Europe and the Pacific, aided by atomic technology. Los Angeles *Examiner* headlines told the final outcome:

"ATOMIC BOMB WIPES OUT 60 PCT OF JAPANESE CITY; Over Four Square Miles [of Hiroshima] 'Destroyed,' Army Reveals." (August 8, 1945)

"2ND ATOM BOMB HITS JAPS; RUSS ATTACK MANCHUKUO. 'All Living Things' [in Nagasaki] Killed, Says Tokyo. Heavy Concrete Air Shelters Pulverized; Cabinet Meets." (August 9, 1945)

"WAR KEEPS GOING. JAPS SILENT ON PEACE. ALLIES BLAST TOKYO." (August 13, 1945)

"JAPS ACCEPT PEACE!" (August 14, 1945)

"VICTORY: WAR IS ENDED!" (August 15, 1945)

At the end of that week, an Oakland mother described her elation at the news to her daughter, who was serving in the Navy WAVES (Women Accepted for Volunteer Emergency Services). That Tuesday, August 14, she went to "look for some stockings, and when I came out from Capwell's, people were throwing paper out of the windows from the Ray Building, and a few minutes after, the *Tribune* Tower siren went off with a blast, and then people went wild. I was so thrilled I almost cried."

The following Sunday, her husband wrote, "is really a day to give thanks, but also one of sorrow for the people who have lost their loved ones. Mom and I," he added, "are loafing around, sipping, or I should say, guzzling ale and watching the passing parade around Lake Merritt." The end of gas rationing brought further enjoyment, and Mom added, "It is a grand and glorious feeling to be able to say, 'fill her up.'"

On September 2, a naval officer wrote a young cousin in Berkeley: "Hi-ya, Ricky: Entered Tokyo Bay this morning, the day of the formal surrender. We are making the first amphibious force landing in Japan. We are anchored off Yokohama, a few miles south of Tokyo, where we have been landing Army troops all day. Wish you could have seen the great show of force as the B-19s and carrier planes flew over the USS *Missouri* this morning following the surrender ceremonies."

THE END OF WORLD WAR II JOLTS CULTURE RADICALLY

With peace came a new world. On the homefront, people burst from the constraints of wartime scarcity; in the world, wartime allies became enemies, as the Cold War began between the United States and the Soviet Union.

California's population and status increased, with many Americans migrating to the west and south, the Sun Belt expansion. In 1958, Major League Baseball eclipsed the 1903 Pacific League when two teams came west from New York City: the San Francisco Giants and the Los Angeles Dodgers.

187

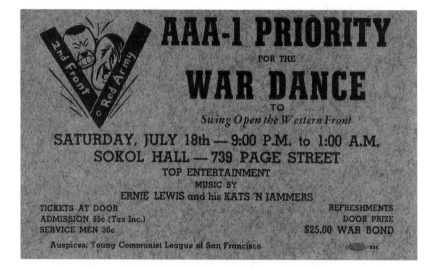

War makes strange allies. In 1942, San Francisco's Young Communists raised money to relieve pressure on beleaguered Russians. Within the next decade, Cold War San Franciscans feared such sympathies.

Two years later, Fred Kohner added another ingredient, surfing, to California's image in his novel *Gidget* (a contraction of "girl midget"), based on his daughter Kathy's escapades. Star Sandra Dee's fantastically successful 1959 movie adaptation sparked this new national fascination with California. In 1961, the Beach Boys began singing of cars, sun, surf, and sex. Naturally, "California Girls" were the best the world could provide. In 1969, Hoyle Schweitzer launched windsurfing when he mounted a rider-controlled sail on a large surfboard. Parents, of course, wondered just what their wild, unchaperoned teenagers were doing.

Other subcultures, such as the Beat literary movement, flourished in California. In 1945, Lawrence Ferling, a young naval officer, visited devastated Nagasaki, tramping through the human remains. Right there, he adopted the anarchist principle that humans are basically good and do not need a heavy-handed government to rule over them. In 1953, after reclaiming the family name, Ferlinghetti joined Peter D. Martin, the son of an Italian anarchist assassinated in New York City, to open a small, pie-shaped bookshop in San Francisco on Columbus Avenue, near Broadway. Named after Martin's literary magazine, which in turn carried the title of a Charlie Chaplin movie where man matched wits with machinery (picture the comic fussing atop a huge gear), City Lights became the first paperback bookshop in the nation. The two proprietors took advantage of the quality titles beginning to appear cheaply in soft cover.

Following a European tradition of bookmaking, City Lights began publishing in 1955. It quickly became, as its sales receipts say, "a literary meeting place," and home of the Beats, or beatniks, as *Chronicle* columnist Herb Caen dubbed them. The best known of the anti-authoritarian, free-flowing Beat, as in "exhausted," writers is Jack Kerouac. In 1957, City Lights' fourth publication, poet Allen Ginsberg's "Howl," expanded

City Lights Books remained closed on March 20, 2003, the first day of war with Iraq. Pointedly, its red banners read, "Stop War and War Makers," with the latter banner showing the likeness of President George W. Bush. In June, proprietors Lawrence Ferlinghetti and Nancy Peters celebrated the institution's fiftieth anniversary. (Photograph by author.)

First Amendment boundaries for the nation. The famed bookstore continues to be a mecca for leftist and offbeat writings.

The pace of social change increased during the 1950s and 1960s. In 1953 in Chicago, Hugh Hefner began publishing *Playboy*. Four years later, the sexual revolution became prominent when Searle introduced the female contraceptive Enovid, otherwise known as "the pill." Then the 1960s brought social and political upheaval. The Reverend Doctor Martin Luther King Jr. led the civil rights movement, drawing radicals and social reformers from California campuses. The assassination of President John F. Kennedy in 1963 vaporized a dream of Camelot, fostering disillusion.

The University of California Campus at Berkeley became the flashpoint and saw the emergence, in journalistic parlance, of the leftist "People's Republic of Beserkeley." In late 1964, the Free Speech Movement brought student power, as Mario Savio led protestors to vanquish a Regents' ban on radical speakers. Frustration over the widening war in Vietnam under Lyndon Baines Johnson in 1965 greatly spread societal change. "Hell, No! We won't go!" greeted the military conscription of soldiers, or "the draft." Throughout the United States, protesters battled police, captured campuses, and welcomed the president with shouts of "Hey! Hey! LBJ! How many kids did you kill today?"

The 1968 assassinations of the Reverend Doctor King and Democratic presidential candidate Robert F. Kennedy, and the following election of Californian Richard Nixon brought tension to a new high. Gradually and painfully, Nixon withdrew from Southeast Asia. When Saigon, now Ho Chi Minh City, fell to the Communists in 1975, many Vietnamese, Laotians, and Cambodians joined California's ethnic mix.

Beginning with 1960, Timothy Leary, through connections to the Beats, advocated the psychedelic drug LSD (lysergic acid diethylamide; the initials come from the German spelling) and other hallucinogens. Forget the world, Leary said, and

191

"Turn on, tune in, and drop out." At Jefferson Airplane or Grateful Dead rock music concerts, such as those promoted by Chet Helms at the Avalon Ballroom and Bill Graham at Fillmore West, the sweet smell of marijuana smoke filled the atmosphere. Free love, or sex without consequences for men and women, blossomed; flower children, other-worldly, back-to-nature types, appeared; experiments in communal living emerged, and appropriate art, music, fashion, and grooming developed to accompany them.

San Francisco became a center for hippies, those colorfully dressed, societal drop-outs, radicals, and antiwar protestors. The cross streets Haight and Ashbury glowed in the embrace of 1967's Summer of Love, when peace and nonviolence would conquer the world. The psychedelic art and articles of the weekly *Oracle* told all. To the south in 1962, at coastal hot springs at Big Sur, Richard Price and Michael Murphy, drawing on East Indian spirituality, launched the Esalen Institute and the human potential movement, or individual self-development and awareness.

By the 1970s, the women's movement was in full swing. With the contraceptive pill, biology was no longer destiny, and women freely entered the workforce. Currently, two-thirds of Wells Fargo Bank's employees are women, and the Bay Area has sent three remarkable ones to Congress—Senators Diane Feinstein and Barbara Boxer, and House of Representatives Democratic Whip Nancy Pelosi.

ELEMENTS OF CALIFORNIA LIFE: TELEVISION, FOOD, WINE, HOUSING, AND FINANCE

Concurrently, elements of the good life emerged as particularly Californian. Hollywood and television became synonymous; TV's "goodness" is still debatable.

From motion pictures, the step was short to television. Californians invented it—San Franciscan Philo T. Farnsworth in 1927, aided with a loan from Crocker Bank, and Harry Lubcke of Los Angeles in 1931, determined the mechanism. Not until after World War II did TV take off through commercial broadcasting stations. California's stations comprised KTLA in Los Angeles in 1947; San Francisco's KPIX in 1948; and San Diego's KFMB in 1950. Of course, the center of the TV world was always New York, but Hollywood jumped into production. *Dragnet*, based on Los Angeles police cases, and the situation comedy *I Love Lucy* quickly pleased audiences, and Westerns, such as *Death Valley Days* and *Tales of Wells Fargo*, followed. Of course, with only black-and-white viewing available, the good guys wore white hats; the outlaws, black. The year 1955 brought Walt Disney's legendary Mouseketeers and early color programming. Americans made TV a part of their daily routine, and by 1966, all programming was in color.

Many shows were half-hour, commercial-studded serials, daily or weekly, training viewers to tune in at the same time, same station. After all, beginning in 1947, the kids in the Peanut Gallery knew what time it was: "It's Howdy Doody Time!" Buffalo Bob brought out the loveable puppet for all the nation to see, while Chief Thunderthud shouted "Cowabunga!"

Vineyard Harvest

Golden State food and wine also gained international renown. In 1971 Berkeley's Alice Waters invented California Cuisine. Her restaurant, Chez Panisse, created menus daily, using the finest local ingredients on hand to determine entrées.

What is good food without good wine? Prohibition crushed the California wine industry, but after suitable aging, its vintage improved. Ernest and Julio Gallo of Modesto began making common wine in huge amounts in 1933, and by 1941 they marketed their own brands. They literally positioned their wines in markets by securing shelf space at eye level. While the Gallo scientific labs refined production, their other facilities investigated practical matters. For instance, the Gallos discovered that green glass filters out taste-harming ultraviolet rays. The brothers had a knack for discerning the tastes of American drinkers, and constantly produced the same quality. By the mid-1960s, E. & J. Gallo led America's wine production.

Many declare that Robert Mondavi inaugurated modern winemaking in 1966 when he began making wine characterized by particular grapes, harvest, and production. He determined to make Napa Valley's wines the best in the world, and in 1976, California wines defeated French ones in a blind tasting at Paris. Now, with each coastal valley producing its own varietals aged in French oak barrels, California vintages are savored around the world—$14 billion worth in 2002.

An Affordable Place to Live

Between 1940 and 1970, the Golden State's population surged to 13 million; in 1962, it became the most populous state in the Union. The California Dream included owning one's own home, and of course, developers produced new suburbs and subdivisions. One-story Californio ranch houses, with informal interiors, wood and stucco construction evolved into mass-produced "California ranch-style" homes. Equally predictably, someone protested. Inspired by the new Daly City in 1962, Malvina Reynolds sang satirically of "ticky-tacky" suburbs. However, they were affordable.

In the Bay Area, Joseph Eichler Homes, Inc. built eleven thousand mass-produced tract homes, which in 1950 sold for only $9,500 each. Based on his experience living in a house

California offered the world affordable homes, whether in the south's hot Imperial Valley or in North Berkeley. "Boulevard Gardens, with quick access to public transportation," was in 1907 "where $50 buys a quarter acre garden plot, and $10 monthly pays the ($1,000) balance." Agents declared, "Get a map, get a car, get a look, and you will get a lot."

designed by Frank Lloyd Wright, Eichler developed a clean, modern design with a glassed atrium that brought the outside in. Eichler houses remain popular today. Similarly, in 1940s Los Angeles, Fritz B. Burns followed the example of flamboyant 1920s builder and promoter Henry Culver. Allied with versatile industrialist Henry J. Kaiser, Burns ultimately produced twelve thousand affordable subdivision homes using prefabrication, mass production, and uniform plans.

Credit Card Borrowing Fuels a Prosperous Economy

Postwar rationing gave way to a huge demand for consumer goods and housing, and customers regularly used their local branch banks. So many households had acquired checking accounts that in 1956, banks, led by Bank of America, introduced checks imprinted with MICR (Magnetic Ink Check Recognition)—the number at the bottom of all checks—to facilitate payments nationwide. Machines read the ink, sorted checks by issuing banks, and routed them back to customers.

The 1960s brought an increase in statewide banks. Since the late 1920s, Bank of America branches covered the entire state. North-south mergers added another two in the early 1960s: Security Pacific Bank of Los Angeles (1960) and Crocker-Citizens Bank of San Francisco (1963). An alarmed state bank superintendent forbade Wells Fargo Bank to do the same thing, so at the close of 1967, it opened a branch in Los Angeles. To escape state regulation altogether, the next year Wells Fargo switched to a national charter.

Credit cards also symbolized the new era. In 1958, Bank of America became the first in the United States to issue a card offering revolving credit (customers could pay off the balance immediately, or in interest-charged installments). In 1966, it began licensing this BankAmericard to other banks (under the VISA name). In response, the next year, Wells Fargo and other banks launched Master Charge (now Mastercard). In the mid-1970s, Crocker Bank became the first California bank to use Automated Teller Machines on a large scale, and by 1980, ATMs were a fact of daily life.

The years 1980 to 1982 brought the chaos of bank deregulation, leading to a prime rate borrowing of 21 percent interest. Deregulation also brought a fraudulent boom of real-estate financing, symbolized by a $2 billion federal bailout of Charles Keating's Los Angeles Lincoln Savings and Loan. New laws also dissolved the barriers between savings and commercial banks, allowing the formerly differently regulated banks to enter into new businesses. The vicissitudes of the economy did not prevent misjudgments by well-run and highly regarded banks. In 1986 The Crocker Bank was bought by Wells Fargo, while in 1992 Security-Pacific became part of Bank of America.

Additionally, changes in federal law permitted interstate banking for the first time in a century, and in the 1990s, California banks aggressively pursued it. However, in 1997, Bank of America vanished into NationsBank of Charlotte, North Carolina, and the next year, Wells Fargo fell prey to Norwest Bank of Minneapolis, Minnesota; only the names survived. Public reaction, though, to closing branches and impersonal electronic transactions in the 1980s brought new conveniences in the 1990s including bank branches in supermarkets, longer hours, 24-hour phone service, and banking over the Internet.

In 1950, San Francisco had a bustling port, boasting banking, insurance, printing, and coffee as its main industries. Fifty years later, shipping, printing, and coffee had vanished, while the others were weaker. Oakland and Los Angeles aggressively picked up seaborne commerce. The European-owned Fireman's Fund (1863) and Transamerica Insurance (1928) exist in the

Bay Area, while Wells Fargo Bank (1852) and the Union Bank of California (1864) are the largest banks headquartered in the Bay City. "Conglomeration" and "online" are the watchwords of business today; geography no longer matters.

RACIAL POLITICS AND URBAN COMPLEXITY

Large groups of twentieth century immigrants from foreign lands arrived in California to labor in the vast agricultural fields. Black Californians have a different story. American-born, they came to work in urban industry. From small nineteenth-century beginnings, California's black population grew rapidly during the twentieth century. The former century saw the Bay Area as the center; the latter a greater gathering in Southern California.

Los Angeles Becomes a Haven for African Americans

In 1902, Los Angeles promoter Jefferson L. Edmunds trumpeted, "California is the greatest state for the Negro." Why? Freedom from lynching, which was common in the South at this time. By 1913, Los Angeles had a chapter of the National Association for the Advancement of Colored People, and one emerged in Oakland in 1915.

Both southern and northern California chapters of the NAACP fought the screening of director David W. Griffith's technologically innovative but racist film, *Birth of a Nation,* based on Thomas Dixon's 1905 novel, *The Clansman: An Historical Romance of the Ku Klux Klan.* As the son of a Confederate colonel, Griffith's bias concerning the post-Civil War South became obvious in this twelve-reel epic.

In this first great masterpiece of movie production, Griffith commanded twenty thousand troops for battle reenactments, which would have made him a major general in the real war, and developed artistic camera angles and superb editing. From its Los Angeles opening on February 8, 1915, "The Birth of a Nation" set world attendance records in spite of a hefty $2 admission fee.

Yet, its message was horrid. A program for Clune's Auditorium Theatre, where the movie premiered, stated the theme: "Insolent power" arising from the "dreams of negro [its spelling] equality" during Reconstruction led to "negro lawlessness" and clashes "with the Aryan race." In character, blacks were brutal rapists—though played by white actors. No wonder African Americans protested!

Los Angeles, as a non-union town, looked favorably on black employees; a 1926 survey showed that 50 out of 456 factories hired African Americans. The Los Angeles Police Department also followed suit. In 1919, Frederick M. Roberts arrived at the California State Assembly.

However, in 1919, the U.S. Supreme Court upheld property restrictions that barred housing sales to African Americans, and did not remove them until 1948 and 1953. Segregated areas led to compact vibrant communities with active cultural lives, including jazz music. In 1923, an eastern paper heralded Watts in Los Angeles as "the coming town of California." Through the Depression, another twenty-four thousand migrants arrived, and the 1930s saw a switch in political allegiance. "Lincoln Freed Us, but Roosevelt Feeds Us," summed up the Democratic party's triumph.

World War II is Decisive

By 1940, California's 125,000 African Americans composed 2 percent of the state's population. In 1940, Los Angeles had

64,000 African Americans, and over 100,000 in 1945; 8,400 called Oakland home in 1940, and 22,000 did so in 1945; nearby Richmond gained 15,000 during the same war period.

World War II brought increased demand for cheap labor. Since the flow of international immigrants was halted, American black men and women took the opportunity. Southern California offered aviation factories, while Northern California was a center of shipbuilding. The new arrivals from the rural South, largely from Texas, battled for a "Double V"—victory over fascism abroad and racism at home.

"Fight or be slaves!" Cottrell Laurence Dellums roared in 1925, when he helped found the Brotherhood of Sleeping Car Porters in Oakland. The son of a Texas slave, he knew of what he spoke. In 1941, Dellums was one of those black leaders nationwide who threatened a march on Washington if employment opportunities did not increase. In response, President Roosevelt issued Executive Order 8802 ending discrimination in federal contracts and defense plants as well as establishing a Committee on Fair Employment Practices.

Even in the armed forces, which the government segregated by race, black Americans found themselves assigned to the least wanted and most dangerous work. The best illustration is the accidental explosion of two ammunition ships on July 17, 1944, at Port Chicago, Contra Costa County, now a National Monument. The fireball, three miles in area and equal in power to the atomic bomb that vaporized Hiroshima, killed 322 men. Two-thirds were black ammunition loaders; their deaths contributed 15 percent of black casualties during the war.

After the war, blacks were the last hired and first fired. Not until 1970 did the first African American reach statewide office, Superintendent of Public Instruction Wilson Riles. Constant discouragement across a wide variety of life activities fueled a mentality that currently considers education "acting white," and presents a lack of alternatives to crime that has placed in jail one of every eleven adult black men in California.

Los Angeles Burns

In 1950, African Americans in California totaled 460,000, or 4 percent of the state's population, with 170,000 living in Los Angeles, and 48,000 in Oakland, where they comprised 12 percent of the East Bay Area's residents. In Brown v. The Topeka Board of Education, the U.S. Supreme Court ruled in 1954 that separate schools for black children were not equal schools, overturning its 1896 Plessy v. Ferguson decision. Such a positive outcome encouraged optimism. In the following decade, African Americans grew from 900,000 to 1,400,000, comprising 8 percent of all Californians.

In the early 1960s, the strains of the civil rights movement anthem "We Shall Overcome" reached the West Coast. The Los Angeles Committee of Racial Equality (CORE) protested segregated schools and housing discrimination in 1963, and Thomas Bradley became the first African American city councilman. In Northern California that same year, William Byron Rumford, a Berkeley assemblyman since 1948, authored a law banning housing discrimination. This was overturned by initiative in 1964, but the U.S. Supreme Court restored justice in 1967. In 1964, Black Studies programs began to emerge at colleges and universities, and in San Francisco, Mayor Jack Shelley appointed the first African American, Terry A. Francois, to the city and county Board of Supervisors.

By the 1960s, though, Watts, the original entry port for black migrants, had long become a term of derision. Too many poor, uneducated immigrants had reduced its charm, and in 1965, South Central Los Angeles exploded in fire. Rumors spread of police brutality after a highway patrolman made a routine drunk-driving arrest. This angered residents, who vented their rage by destroying their own neighborhood. Watts burned for six days in August heat, as ten thousand rioted, murdered, looted, and destroyed white businesses. The Watts Riot was the most destructive in American history.

Southern Californian Ron Karenga offered one way out of despondency through founding US in 1965. Fluent in Swahili, a language of East Africa, Karenga took a Swahili name, Maulana. Drawing from the South African Zulus, he created a unifying philosophy and community ceremonies emphasizing pride and self-help. These principles are celebrated in the holiday of Kwanzaa, a Christmastime festival adopted in 1966 and recognized in a 1997 postage stamp. The holiday continually grows in popularity nationwide.

Less than a decade later, the City of Angels had its first black mayor. Thomas Bradley left the city council in 1973 to enter the first of five terms as mayor (1973–1993). He also ran for governor in 1982 and 1986. He had to deal with many difficult issues as mayor, including air pollution. In 1945, after thirty-five years, the Pacific Electric's Big Red Cars began their final decline. Back in 1910, their twelve hundred miles of track linked fifty communities through the Los Angeles basin in the world's largest electric mass-transit system. What was the replacement for rapid-rail transit? Smog-belching automobiles, along with a network of freeways and interchanges, created by a road-building decree of the 1959 state legislature.

The 1960 legislature responded to the growing smog problem with the first law in the United States to reduce air pollution. It established a standards-setting Air Resources Board, and after 1966, it required cars to have smog-control devices. In contrast, Congress did not pass the Clean Air Act laws until 1967 and 1970. Mayor Bradley reaped benefits as air slowly became clearer and cleaner above Los Angeles. In 1984, the legislature made smog inspections mandatory as Los Angeles hosted the Olympics (as the City of Angels had done in 1932).

However, the use of fuel additives to cut pollution has brought mixed results. In 1989, Southern California became the first to have the oxygenate MTBE (Methyl tertiary-butyl ether) added to its gasoline, preceding the 1990 federal Clean Air Act mandating such additives. In spring 1996, MTBE went statewide and the next year, complaints began to roll in—and not just about the 3 to 5 cents additional cost per gallon. MTBE burns clean but spreads rapidly underground, polluting water supplies.

Tom Bradley's final year as mayor, though, was not pleasant. On April 29, 1992, a Simi Valley jury freed four white policemen who had been videotaped beating a black motorist, Rodney King. Anger in South Central Los Angeles erupted immediately against white society in general, and local Korean groceries and liquor stores in particular. Rioters ignored Mayor Bradley's attempts to restore order. The three days of burning chaos left 38 dead and 1,250 injured.

Only African-American enclaves have been torn apart through rioting, and in April 2003, the city council renamed these sixteen square miles. Now less known for drugs and crime, and with an ethnically mixed population, South Central Los Angeles has become South Los Angeles.

Oakland: Radicalism, Idealism, and Confusion

In 1966, Northern California, home to many radical movements, saw the birth of the most extreme version of "Black Power." Its exponents forcefully argued that the future of African Americans lay in their own efforts; white America would give them nothing. They must seize destiny. Oakland residents Huey P. Newton, Bobby Seale, David Hilliard, and Eldridge and Kathleen Cleaver founded the Black Panther Party. Imbued with Marxist radicalism and a hatred of police, members went armed.

"We are a colonial people," Newton declared in January 1968. "We are after full employment, better housing, a decent education, and a share in the wealth of this country." The Panthers also offered free hot breakfasts for schoolchildren, sickle cell anemia testing, housing, and jobs. Bobby Seale's showing in the 1973 mayoral primary shook up the Oakland establishment. However, by the early 1970s, the promise had died. Many of the leaders drifted out of politics. Newton gained control, leading Panther remnants to violence, extortion, and drugs. A drug-fueled decline brought his death in 1989 on the mean streets of West Oakland.

Countering the leftist radicals, attorneys and other professional black men and women ran for office in Oakland. To gain credibility, the first generation of a political movement must appeal to the general public good. In 1977, Lionel Wilson, a superior court judge, became mayor, while African Americans gained the city council. Meantime, industry left Oakland for Mexico and elsewhere, while Wilson formed alliances with developers and dispensed patronage to get projects completed. As president of the board of Port Commissioners in the 1970s, attorney Thomas L. Berkeley, publisher of the Oakland *Post*, and a co-founder of the West Coast Black Publishers Association, led the conversion to automated container-loading operations. Cranes swinging aboard huge boxes of cargo replaced gangs of stevedores.

The 1980s brought additional difficulties to Oakland. A crack cocaine epidemic raged, particularly among the poor African American neighborhoods; the 7.1 Richter Scale Loma Prieta earthquake on October 17, 1989, cracked the business district tax base; and the October 20, 1991, Oakland Hills fire killed twenty-five and incinerated about three thousand residences. Assemblyman Elihu Harris succeeded Wilson as mayor in 1990, but instead of introducing reforms, he gained a reputation as a poor administrator, known for backroom deals and a bloated bureaucracy.

As the decade wore on, progressives moved out, the black middle class disappeared as a political force, and in 1998 Jerry Brown, former "Governor Moonbeam" (1975–1983), so designated for his unrealistic, flaky proposals, ended African American dominance. Brown also has the advantage of an initiative legislating a strong mayor.

With blacks down to a third of the population, Oakland is now a much more racially mixed city, although tragically, murder in poor, black neighborhoods is seen as commonplace— a record 113 in 2002, and 100 by mid-October 2003. "Sadly," the San Francisco *Chronicle* editorialized on this last tombstone, "it shocked practically no one." Using Oakland's population of 412,000 in 2003, this presents a homicide ratio of 27 per 100,000 in 2002, and a rate of 30 per 100,000 so far in 2003.

By 2003, Mayor Brown and the African-American city manager Robert Bobb brought revival with new business and a war against crime and grime. Good things always end; this partnership did on July 1, when Mayor Brown unceremoniously sacked the city manager to take more direct charge of affairs. "After decades of government ineptness and development miscues," the *Chronicle* editorially opined, "Bobb got things done."

San Francisco, "The City that Knows How"

Across the bay from Oakland is San Francisco. In 2002, the population for the city and county of San Francisco had declined

205

to 765,000. African Americans are moving to affordable homes in the suburbs, and white men and women are gentrifying the city. Meantime, the municipal workers union has a stranglehold over city government, whose labyrinthine bureaucracy and city council antics often resemble a circus. The growing homeless population embarrasses all.

For eight years, another African-American politician has made his mark. In 1996, Willie Brown, for fifteen years the record-holding Speaker of the Assembly (1980–1995), became "Da Mayor." When in the legislature, Speaker Brown described himself as "Ayatollah of the Assembly." Shrewd to the point of genius, Brown used his immense political talents to reward friends, humiliate enemies, collect girlfriends, and broker deals. In reaction to his high-handed boldness, the 1992 initiative imposing term limits on the legislature might as well be called the "Brown Act."

As mayor of San Francisco, Brown made race-based appointments and supported black candidates, with mediocre results. Only the ability of the superintendent of schools has stood out among the assessor, election commissioner, fire chief, municipal railway officers, police chief, public housing officials, and supervisors. Too often the cry of "racism" greets any critique of performance, accusations of favoritism, or of a mentality that equates victimization with entitlement. Now, population demographics have bypassed African Americans.

As Willie Brown's term as mayor draws to a close, the daily San Francisco *Chronicle* foresees a poor legacy. A headline on April 4 announced, "Treasure Island Project Expected to go to Mayor's Cronies: Huge Development Lacked Competition, According to Critics." On April 11, 2003, a news story elaborated on this: "Two leading financial backers of San Francisco Mayor Willie Brown and other state Democrats have secured exclusive rights to negotiate a deal to develop the former Navy base at Treasure and Yerba Buena Islands." The *Chronicle* on July 15 editorially denounced the "flagrant flaunting of ethics" and "the low ethical standards set by Brown's administration." On September 28, 2003, it condemned city hall's "odorous corruption and cronyism."

Rebellion reared in 2000, when a return to separate elections for the eleven supervisor districts brought a factionalized but anti-Brown board. Audacity worthy of Brown himself came on October 22, 2003, when the mayor was in Tibet. Acting Mayor Chris Daly, "the brat boy of the left," to appropriate the *Chronicle's* terminology, appointed and swore in two avid environmentalists to the five-member Public Utilities Commission board that is overseeing the reconstruction of the Hetch Hetchy water system.

Yet, no one can top Da Mayor for elegant appearance, commanding presence, quick wit, and political ability. His flamboyance advertises the City by the Bay wherever he goes. In addition to being a good friend of developers, Mayor Brown instituted the Municipal Railway's Third Street light-rail extension. Matching Willie Brown in class is a project he made happen: Elegant Pacific Bell Park, since 2000 the home of San Francisco Giants baseball.

NEW INGREDIENTS FLAVOR THE POLITICAL STEW

Just as African American men and women vigorously flexed political muscles, two other formerly quiet groups have come to actively seek office. Homosexuals have a primarily urban base in San Francisco and Los Angeles, while Latinos, so far, are strong in the south.

Gay Pride

Beginning in the 1970s, a new political element emerged when the San Francisco homosexual, or gay, community became a vibrant force. Assemblyman Brown led the charge to decriminalize homosexual sexual behavior. In 1977, district elections made abrasive Harvey Milk the first avowed gay on a board of supervisors anywhere. When gunshots from renegade supervisor Dan White martyred Milk and Mayor George Moscone on November 27, 1978, the gay and lesbian community exploded with energy. In June 1979, Gilbert Baker's six-striped rainbow flag became the first internationally recognizable gay icon, as the official emblem of San Francisco's sixth Gay Freedom Day Parade. Homosexuals came out of the closet and into the streets.

San Francisco, with 2 percent of all couples, has the densest gay population in the nation, followed closely by West Hollywood and Palm Springs. The Golden State, with ninety-two thousand reported couples holds 20 percent of the nation's total. A U.S. Supreme Court decision on June 26, 2003, striking down a Texas sodomy law, and calling into question sex-based legislation, holds promise for future legal rights. Following Vermont's 2000 lead, on September 19, Governor Gray Davis signed the Domestic Partners Rights and Responsibilities Act of 2003 granting many privileges enjoyed by married couples. Same-sex couples gain health insurance coverage, community property, liability for a partner's debts, alimony, and child support; they do not get income and inheritance tax, Social Security, and pension benefits.

Yet a deadly disease carried out of Africa by an airline steward would prove especially devastating for the gay community. On June 5, 1981, in Los Angeles, came the first diagnosis of Acquired Immune Deficiency Syndrome (AIDS). It wiped out nineteen thousand San Franciscans, a generation of

More than 160 groups marched jovially in the thirty-third Gay Pride Parade on June 29, 2003. "You Gotta Give Them Hope" was the slogan of Supervisor Harvey Milk, assassinated twenty-five years previously. Just prior to the 2003 parade, the United States Supreme Court struck down a Texas sodomy law. Signs at the parade read, "We All Deserve the Freedom to Marry." While men dance on a float, a rainbow flag waves in the background. (Photograph by author's daughter.)

gays. Worldwide, where deaths have amounted to 20 million in twenty years, AIDS has not discriminated in its victims; in the United States its first victims were gay men and intravenous drug users. Today, the disease has migrated into the mainstream American population. About two-thirds of national new cases strike minorities. In the last twenty years, some 450,000 Americans have died of AIDS. The human immunodeficiency virus (HIV), which causes AIDS, currently can be somewhat controlled, but not cured, by a cocktail of drugs. People with HIV now have the ability to live relatively normal lives for many years. Public health campaigns now encourage all Americans to practice safe sexual behavior.

Latinos: California's Largest Minority

As the twentieth century began, the great majority of Spanish-speaking immigrants arrived from Mexico, congregating in Southern California urban barrios. By 1940, the majority society generally considered them, as one teacher said, "dirty, stupid and dumb." In an effort to gain respect, beginning in the 1940s, teenagers in East Los Angeles flaunted their differences. The Zoot Suit, an outlandish outfit, became the uniform of protest. It comprised an extremely long, large lapelled coat, baggy trousers worn high and cuffed at the ankles, and a "duck tail" haircut. A minority went further than merely mocking authority, adopting the aimless violence of the irrational "la vida loca." The Zoot Suit phenomenon of the early 1940s became a prelude to the public display of countercultural values through dress as practiced by white hippies and radicals in the 1960s.

Brawls and clashes with the police and servicemen became common enough to spark a fear of a "Mexican crime wave," which erupted in pitched battles between sailors and Zoot

Suiters, in which the servicemen were the aggressors, between June 3 and June 10, 1943. Attacked and defensive, Mexican Americans united. One lasting result was the emergence of a violent gang culture that still exists today.

Through the 1930s, Okies (poor whites from the prairie states, particularly Oklahoma) were often the farm laborers of choice, until World War II sucked them into industry and the army. At first, from World War II to 1964, "Braceros," temporary workers from Mexico, filled the void. As the Bracero program ended in scandal over the mistreatment of these agricultural and railroad laborers, other Mexican laborers came over the border. César Chavez, a former migrant worker, united in 1965 with Larry Itliong's striking Filipino grape laborers at Delano. The next year, Chavez marched on Sacramento, formed the United Farm Workers union, and began a five-year successful national grape boycott. The poorly paid 20 percent of the Hispanic population that labored in California's rich, vast agricultural fields formed his union's core.

Thirty-five years made all the difference in this agricultural labor struggle. In the 1930s, the Salinas Valley furnished three-quarters of domestically grown lettuce. In 1936 growers crushed unionization among Mexican and Filipino harvesters of this delicate, time-sensitive crop. In 1970 the results were different. A strike in the Salinas Valley and boycotts of lettuce brought contracts, higher hourly wages, and benefits. Five years later in 1975, Governor Jerry Brown's pioneering Agricultural Labor Relations Act gave farm workers the right to organize.

Since the mid-1980s, though, the fire has gone from the agricultural workers' movement. Some eighty farm labor contractors have taken over procuring workers for growers, resulting in lower hourly wages and no benefits. Although the charismatic Chavez became honored with a holiday and

211

postage stamp, and co-founder Dolores Huerta remains very much active, the United Farm Workers is moribund. Furthermore, the 1994 North American Free Trade Agreement (NAFTA) between Mexico, the United States, and Canada has driven lower-paying jobs to Mexico.

Through the 1940s, prejudice had always rankled. California Latinos won the first federal court rulings stating that separate schools were not equal. In 1944, Gonzalo and Felicitas Mendez leased an Orange County ranch owned by interred Japanese Americans. When the neighboring school refused to admit their three young children, the Mendez family sued. In February 1946, Los Angeles Federal District Judge Paul McCormick ruled that "regardless of lineage" the public schools must be "open to all children." Governor Earl Warren and attorney Thurgood Marshall supported Judge McCormick when the Westminster School District appealed to the Ninth Circuit Court. This court upheld the decision in 1947. In 2001 Santa Ana named a school after the Mendez family.

In the 1960s, urban Mexican Americans joined with other groups revolting against white dominance, and M.E.Ch.A (Movimiento Estudiantil Chicano de Aztlan) emerged in 1969 at the University of Santa Barbara. Flourishing on college campuses, it advocated reclaiming "Aztlan," the territory the United States gained after the Mexican War (Texas, Arizona, New Mexico, and California) and returning it to Mexico. They spouted an exclusionary motto: "Por La Raza todo. Fuera de La Raza nada," or, "For Chicanos everything; for others, nothing." Such discrimination mirrored the distinction eighteenth-century Spanish colonizers made between the "people of reason," themselves, and those without, the Indians.

In 1960s M.E.Ch.A, Fresno-born Cruz M. Bustamante got a taste for politics and ran for office. In 1996, he became the first Hispanic speaker of the California State Assembly; in 1998, the

212

first Latino lieutenant governor since Romaldo Pacheco in 1871; and in 2003, he was the leading Democrat in contention to replace the recalled governor Gray Davis.

In the United States since 1980, the number of Latinos jumped by a margin of 1.5 to 39 million, and they have just edged out African Americans as the largest national minority. Los Angeles politics are on the verge of acknowledging that Latinos are the largest minority in California. In June 2001, James Hahn became mayor, receiving four times as many black votes as his opponent, Antonio Villaraigosa. For forty years as a county supervisor, Hahn's father Kenneth had legendarily represented the African-American community.

While he made a strong showing, Villaraigosa, with an undistinguished record as Assembly Speaker, could not quite pull off victory. A former M.E.Ch.A member of the 1960s, he is attuned to Mexican problems and advocates rights for illegal immigrants. San Diego, though, may become the first city in California to be governed by a Latino. Mexican culture permeates the region, and it is the primary place of entry for immigrants.

These illegal immigrants from Mexico spark a political flashpoint. A constant influx of Hispanics over the long, porous Mexican border keeps urban and agricultural wages low, rights suppressed, and social services uncertain. Yet, as American watchfulness increases along the border, illegals stay in California rather than tempting danger, seizure, and the expense of a skilled guide to cross the national boundaries. The more who stay underground, the greater the increase on tax-payer funded services. Proposition 187, passed overwhelmingly in 1994 with 60 percent of the vote, but judicially emasculated, would have denied heath care and schooling to these people.

Furthermore, both legal and illegal Mexican-born residents, who form 45 percent of California's workforce, have their

213

own particular problems. Poor English skills and low educational levels dampen upward mobility; 30 percent drop out of high school, compared to 13 percent of blacks and 7 percent of whites.

This growing Mexican-born population has spurred academic study of Chicano literature, history, and culture. In 1966, the Oakland Library opened its Latin American branch (now named for César Chavez), the first in the nation for this specific group. In 2003, the Chicano Studies Department at California State University at Northridge, one of nineteen nationally, is larger than the departments of history, political science, sociology, and foreign languages combined. The University of California, Santa Barbara intends to offer doctorates in Chicano Studies in 2004, while the University of California, Los Angeles contemplates a similar course.

CALIFORNIA'S CONSTANT FERMENT: ECONOMY VERSUS ENVIRONMENT

During the nineteenth century, placer mining was the huge land destroyer. Miners got at gravel gold by diverting rivers, blasting away hillsides with hard jets of water, leaving the debris to clog rivers and flood land downstream, and deep plowing flatlands with huge dredges that left rock in their wakes. In the late twentieth and early twenty-first centuries, the environmental struggle is no longer gold versus grain, but is more intricately involved in all citizens' daily lives.

Santa Clara Valley prunes were famous the world over. Now at night, lights shine densely across the valley's width. The computer age brought an economic boom, but banished agriculture. The Armed Forces also claimed large tracts of land. However, with the Department of Defense closing bases and draining large sums from the California economy, former bases are currently available for business development—or preservation as needed open space. The Golden Gate National Recreation Area and the Presidio of San Francisco are two examples.

Modern civilization runs on electricity, from household appliances to computers, and Californians have a huge electrical appetite. Can the state produce or import enough at affordable costs?

The Miracle of Silicon Valley

Intriguingly, the greedy Southern Pacific Railroad Octopus actually brought about the development of Santa Clara County's "Silicon Valley" (named after the basic ingredient needed for computer chips). Leland Stanford Junior University, designated as a memorial for the son of the railroad president, opened in Palo Alto in 1891. Soon, Stanford University forged an alliance with the growing hydroelectric industry and branched off into radio, microwaves, and other electric research.

Frederick E. Terman, a professor of electrical engineering from the 1920s through the 1960s, was the catalyst for the digital revolution. In 1939, two of Terman's students, William Hewlett and David Packard, started an electronics firm in a Palo Alto garage—which the state fifty years later designated as the "birthplace of Silicon Valley." In 1966, Hewlett-Packard would produce its first mainframe computer, and in 1968, the first desktop computer.

After World War II, Terman brought in government research money, and in 1956, Nobel Prize winner William B. Schockley, the father of the transistor, set up the first semiconductor company. His employees shortly spun off into Fairchild Semiconductor. The amoeba-like company kept splitting, reproducing, and forming new companies.

215

Thirty start-ups appeared between 1968 and 1971. In the fall of 1968, Bob Noyce, Gordon E. Moore, and Andy Grove founded Intel. They had moved to California to escape the stifling management of eastern manufacturing. In 1965, Moore promulgated a Law, which said the number of transistors on a chip would double every twelve months. The current version of Moore's Law fixes the time at eighteen months. In 1973, white "bunny suits" ensuring sterile cleanliness during chip production debuted; in 1993, the Pentium microprocessor was developed; and in 2003, the world's foremost chipmaker shipped its one billionth chip.

The Stanford-centered research ferment continued, especially after 1975, in the aptly named Homebrew Computer Club. The following year, another garage became home to Apple Computer. In 1977, four years before IBM's PC, Steve Jobs and Steven Wozniak led the home computer revolution with the Apple II, and ultimately sold 5.5 million of them. The "user-friendly" Macintosh, with its graphic icons and "mouse" controller, made its debut in January 1984.

Through the 1960s, Doug Englebart, yet another Stanford professor, kept inventing necessary components. From his World War II radar work came the computer screen. His fertile brain also gave birth to word processing, the mouse, and hypertext, the linked text used on the World Wide Web.

In 1974, Stanford computer science professor Vint Cerf joined with Bob Kahn, a one-time University of California, Los Angeles, colleague, to write protocols to allow one computer to send information to another. Kahn called his conduits between computers containing packet nets of information "Internetting." Building on a 1989 Swiss scientific sharing computer network, on December 12, 1991, Stanford physicist Paul Kunz linked a large scientific data base to the World Wide Web and created the first web site in the United States. The creation of the Internet sparked a knowledge and communication explosion.

Other start-ups took advantage of this new medium. September 1995 saw Pierre Omidyar develop eBay, the famed worldwide auction house, in his San Jose living room. Out of the Stanford dorm room of Larry Page and Sergey Brin in 1998 came Google, the ubiquitous search engine, with three billion pages of information at its disposal to answer 200 million requests each day.

This kettle kept bubbling until it boiled over—leading to a dot.com explosion in the late 1990s. The pace, reminiscent of that of the "Days of old, the Days of gold, the Days of '49," moved so quickly that few constructed basic business plans, relying on venture capital. In 2000, as with an 1870s mining stock mania, the high-tech boom revealed its shallowness and collapsed. Since 2000, two hundred thousand jobs have vanished, as companies move technology jobs "offshore" to India and elsewhere.

However, the San Jose area Silicon Valley's underlying vitality remains. Based on population numbers, the U.S. Census Department in June 2003 renamed the Bay Area. The designation reversed the order of city names from the San Francisco-San Jose-Oakland Metropolitan Area to the San Jose-San Francisco-Oakland Metropolitan Area.

Defense Dollars Depart

During World War II, the Federal Government spent $35 billion in California. The state's level of funding was third behind New York and the automobile state, Michigan. Personal incomes tripled on average. San Francisco Bay became the world's largest shipyard, employing 300,000, while aircraft factories in the southern part of the state gave work to an additional 280,000 men and women.

217

In the twentieth century, San Diego grew to become California's Navy Town. In the foreground during World War I, crews—two officers and twenty-six men—work on three 154-foot, 1914 K-class submarines. San Francisco's Union Iron Works built three of the eight subs of this class, including the K-8 in the center (circa 1914).

At the Kaiser shipyard in Richmond, prefabrication brought speed. On November 10, 1942, workers launched the Liberty Ship *Robert E. Perry* in only four days. Two weeks after workers laid the keel, the ship headed out into the Pacific. In 2000, this shipyard site became Rosie the Riveter World War II Home Front National Historic Park. It honors those women who entered the workforce temporarily during the war, like "Rosie" in the 1942 hit song. After 1960, California grabbed about 40 percent of all defense dollars.

Federal outlays are still huge for high technology research and development—air, space, and weaponry— and in 2003 these grew by 19 percent in the Bay Area due to the Iraq war. However, this was also the national rate of growth, so California received nothing special. These funds go to professionals at places such as the Lawrence Livermore Laboratory and the Lockheed Martin Corporation, not to a broad segment of population. Measured by military installations supporting thousands of soldiers and civilians who spend paychecks in their communities, defense spending has disappeared from the Bay Area and large areas of the California economy as well.

The 1960s anti-Vietnam War effort centered in San Francisco. In 1970, Ron Dellums, nephew of Oakland labor leader C.L. Dellums, became the second black member of the House of Representatives, and a leading anti-Vietnam War advocate. The Armed Forces took note of the increasingly hostile environment. A longtime officer once remarked to me, "the Army does not go where it is not wanted."

A glimpse of things to come arrived in 1974, when the Navy closed the five-hundred-acre Hunter's Point Naval Shipyard in San Francisco, cutting seventeen thousand jobs. Now the area remains empty, and the surrounding African American neighborhood endures 40 percent unemployment. Thirty years of arguments over $500 million needed for toxic cleanup

219

Southern California desert hills form a backdrop to a Cold War Army anti-aircraft Nike missile battery at Chatsworth, near Los Angeles. The Greek goddess of Victory supplied the name. Introduced in 1954, the liquid-fueled Nike-Ajax (background) had a limited range of 25 miles. In contrast, the Nike-Hercules, shown publicly for the first time here in August 1958, gained a 90-mile range from solid fuel. By 1974, changing missile technology led to deactivation of all 250 sites, but volunteers keep operational a Nike battery at Fort Barry in the Marin Headlands. (Courtesy of the U.S. Army.)

have delayed one thousand new construction jobs, sixteen hundred homes, and three hundred thousand square feet of commercial space.

Beginning in 1988 at the initiative of "peaceful" Ron Dellums as chair of the House Armed Services Committee, and continuing to the present, the Department of Defense closed twenty-nine California military bases, leaving sixty-one in the Golden State. Military personnel dropped from 270,000 to 123,000. California lost 100,000 jobs and $9.6 billion in revenue. Nationwide, four rounds of closure between 1988 and 1995 eliminated 97 installations; 425 remain.

The Bay Area and Sacramento were hardest hit. When Sacramento's McClellan Air Force Base, which hosted twenty-two thousand men during World War II and thirty thousand in the Vietnam War closed, only two remained: Travis in Solano County, and Beale near Marysville. Dellums' Alameda County lost the Alameda Naval Air Station, Oakland Army Base, Oakland Naval Hospital, and the Fleet Industrial Supply Center, totaling ten thousand blue-collar jobs worth $400 million. Now, Alameda Island is gentrified and liberal—with no jobs for laboring men and women.

Other Bay Area departures included Mare Island Naval Shipyard, Treasure Island, the Concord Naval Weapons Center, which supplied the Pacific Fleet, and Onizuka Air Station in Sunnyvale. On October 30, 2002, Fort Baker on the Marin side of the Golden Gate became part of the National Parks Service. Congressman Philip Burton turned the sites of the Bay harbor defenses into the Golden Gate National Recreation Area, providing some benefit to the community.

In all, thirty thousand military jobs and twenty-four thousand civilian ones vanished, ending an economic component of the Bay Area that supplied civilian labor-intensive posts and shipyards, reaching back to over two centuries to March 28, 1776, when Spanish troops established the Presidio.

Southern California had a similar experience. San Bernardino's Norton Air Force Base closed in 1993, deleting ten thousand jobs and a $258 million payroll. A few miles south, the downgrading of Riverside's March Air Force Base to a reserve facility cost nine thousand jobs and $240 million.

Current development proposals at both former bases are mired in lawsuits. Proponents argue that commerce would create fifteen thousand jobs at the Riverside center alone and abolish an Orange County commute for local residents. Opponents counter that a sea of warehouses serviced by smoke-spewing trucks would unleash noise, water, and air pollution.

An alternative is for business to move to George Air Force Base in the high desert near Victorville. The benefits of this option include 43.5 million square feet of industrial space and, due to the vastness of this bleak area, no worries about housing development or truck and train transportation.

California Short-Circuited

In the early 1990s, due to environmental costs, the collapse of nuclear energy, and lack of new power plant construction, Californians paid 50 percent more for electricity than the rest of the nation. On September 23, 1996, Governor Pete Wilson signed a law that produced energy deregulation so convoluted and mismanaged that it drove Pacific Gas & Electric, Southern California Edison, and San Diego Electric into or to the verge of bankruptcy. Greed and corruption not seen since the post Civil War Gilded Age combined to manipulate the spot market, the price at any given moment, for electric power and clean-burning natural gas, which powered the power-producing plants.

The result of this was devastating. On June 14, 2000, Bay Area Californians suffered the worst deliberate blackout since the Second World War. More hardship was to come. On December 15, 2000, the spot electricity market charged

California more than $1,400 per kilowatt for electricity that had cost $45 per kilowatt the previous December. In mid-January 2001, rolling blackouts covered northern and central California.

On March 19–20, 2001, electricity interruptions finally reached energy-consuming Southern California, inconveniencing 1.5 million throughout the state. The state budget surplus vanished in a $10 billion purchase of energy, and customers today pay twice as much as they did before deregulation—but continue to consume it in colossal amounts. Intriguingly, states that deregulated electricity had the highest rates afterward; California, at 14.5 cents per kilowatt-hour, leads them all.

Hope for the Environment: A Constant Battle

World-famous San Francisco Bay and the densely developed counties that surround it exemplify ecological battles throughout California. While the city of San Francisco lives in political turmoil, the Bay faces environmental damage and decline. In 1961, a group of Berkeley women led the charge to save the rapidly filling, increasingly polluted Bay. Before the Bay could become all water lots and filled land, the legislature responded in 1969, by creating the San Francisco Bay Conservation and Development Commission. Comprised of local, state, and federal agencies, it has allowed development while permitting public access to beaches, cutting pollution so that the water no longer stinks, and enlarging the Bay. Travelers flying into the San Francisco airport may soon see the salt evaporation ponds at the south end become wild wetlands again.

However, the purity of the Bay's water has declined recently. First, Los Angeles' insatiable grasp for water stopped the flow of new sediment that buried Gold Rush toxins, while secondly, ocean tides stirred up mercury-laced gold mining debris. While concentrations of the banned insecticide DDT decline, selinium pollution remains high, and flame retardant PBDE has increased. In July 2003, California became the first state to ban this chemical used to slow the burn rate in foam furniture cushions.

Authorities warn against eating more than two meals a month of San Francisco Bay sport fish. Meantime, a rise in water temperature coupled with over-fishing is depleting herring, the last commercial fishery in the Bay. During the fishing season from December to May, eighty boats seek sac roe from female herring for the Japanese market, giving employment to a thousand. Similarly, sturgeon, which grow up to ten feet long in the Bay and Delta, have dropped by half in the past five years to seventy-seven thousand for similar reasons. Russian immigrants poach them for caviar.

Additionally, another form of "illegal immigration" has taken a toll in Bay waters. In the 1970s, environmentalists introduced East Coast cordgrass (*Spartina alterniflora*) to reduce erosion in South Bay salt ponds. As with many other transplantations at first seen as beneficial, this one became destructive. Cordgrass does stop erosion, but by doing so, it elevates mudflats eighteen inches, turns them into dry prairies, and eliminates native Pacific cordgrass. In 1986, the small but prolific Asian clam arrived unbidden and destroyed fishing as it disrupted food supplies for crustaceans and fish. Other biological threats include the Chinese mitten crab, a 1992 colonizer that spread to the Delta in 1996 and soon blocked water-intake screens at pumping stations. The water hyacinth has a similar clogging effect.

CALIFORNIA AND THE INTERNATIONAL ARENA

California now has a population of 35 million. In 2003, it was 2 percent Native American, or 628,000; 6 percent black; 12

percent Asian (of many nationalities); and 30 percent Hispanic, also from many countries but predominantly Mexican. Residents annually increase by 600,000.

As during the Gold Rush a century and a half ago, a great number of these people are not yet integrated into the general society. In 2002, California's 27 percent foreign-born population was the highest of any state, and a rate equaled only a century before. Urban areas registered higher, with the highest concentration being in Southern California: Riverside, 24 percent; San Diego, 28 percent; Long Beach, 31 percent; Anaheim, 40 percent; Los Angeles, 41 percent; and Santa Ana, 48 percent. The Northern California cities with the most foreign-born are Fresno, 23 percent; Stockton, 24 percent; Sacramento, 26 percent; Oakland, 27 percent; and San Jose and San Francisco at 37 percent. In the past, newcomers met denunciation, but now "embrace diversity" is the watchword for a *laissez faire* attitude towards differing cultures. With few universal beliefs or holidays, will multiculturalism bring fragmentation?

In comparison, according to the 2000 Census, the national rate is 11 percent, yet the foreign-born population jumped by 1.6 million between 2001 and 2002, or 5 percent. Between 2000 and 2002, New York City grew from 20 to 36 percent foreign-born, while Miami registered 61 percent immigrant. Of the new Californians, 54 percent speak Spanish, and 34 percent have arrived from Asia. While Chinese comprise the largest number of Asians, with Filipinos a close second, California has the largest number of Vietnamese, 450,000 and 40 percent of those in the United States, living outside of their home country.

Some of these foreign-born must hide, for they have arrived without welcoming papers. In 2000, the United States contained 7 million undocumented immigrants, who entered from China, Mexico, and other Central and South American countries. Of these, 2.2 million or one-third resided in California.

225

Yet, political institutions do not provide solutions. For years, California has faced governmental gridlock. California levies the highest taxes in the nation—income, sales, vehicle, workers compensation—and has little to show for it. Property taxes were in that list until a voters' revolt against a "tax and spend" philosophy on June 6, 1978, rolled them back with Proposition 13. Schooling remains poor, while in the thirty years since Governor Edmund G. "Pat" Brown (1959–1967), California's highways have dropped to dead last in maintenance and development in the nation. With a governor and legislature usually refusing to manage or legislate, government by initiative has become an unsuitable, but actual alternative.

The traditional north-south split between San Francisco and Los Angeles has lessened as western coastal cities, especially San Francisco, become liberal enclaves and eastern hinterlands turn conservative. Statewide, the Republican party, which produced two conservative Presidents, Richard M. Nixon (1969–1974) and Ronald Reagan (1981–1989) has collapsed almost into impotency and irrelevance, while unhappy, feuding Democrats hold all state offices and control the legislature.

However, in California, the unexpected is expected, as implied by the title of a 1949 book by Carey McWilliams, *California: The Great Exception*. A huge deficit, economic collapse, general inaction, lack of leadership, and particular favoritism to special interest groups stoked a demand to recall Governor Gray Davis. On October 7, 2003, more voters turned out for California's first statewide recall than had for any election for governor since 1982. As Democrats moved left politically, moderate Republican Arnold Schwarzenegger terminated three serious rivals. This Austrian-born actor exuded supreme self-confidence during his campaign.

World events have a peculiar way of intruding into California affairs. Today, some portions of this heterogeneous population live under increased national security. With the collapse of the Soviet Union and the end of the Cold War, a new enemy has brought terror and constriction to the nation: the radical Islamic terrorism that produced the attacks of September 11, 2001, on New York City's World Trade Center and the Pentagon in the nation's capital. On September 11, 2001, the world changed for Americans. In response, President George W. Bush inaugurated an aggressive foreign policy, invading Afghanistan and Iraq. Fearing domestic sabotage, the administration pushed the U.S.A. Patriot Act of October 31. This program of national watchfulness and curtailment is in direct descent from four 1798 laws: the Naturalization Act; the Alien Act, the Alien Enemies Act, and the Sedition Act.

This terrorism born of a mix of Middle Eastern politics and Islamic fundamentalism is not new to California. Turmoil and anger from halfway around the world arrived in the Golden State in 1968. On June 5, in Los Angeles, Palestinian Sirhan Sirhan assassinated Democratic Presidential candidate Robert Kennedy, who supported Israel. The technique and results mirror Osama bin Laden's hatred of everything Western. Nor should one forget the California connection to Afghanistan through converted Muslim John Walker Lindh, the "Marin Taliban," captured in December 2001 while serving with enemy forces.

The Golden Gate Bridge.

CONCLUSION

California Today

A cliché states that the more things change, the more they remain the same. The attractiveness of California still draws people. Assimilating different populations has been a constant struggle for the state since the eighteenth century. The resettlement camps of World War II seemed to have purged the California mind of a Japanese menace, while within the past twenty years, the African American population stabilized. Current immigration concentrates on Asians and Latinos, a continuation of absorption begun two centuries ago. The strife between national unity and ethnic fragmentation continues.

Social problems concerning the down and out goes on, but incorporate Marxist, leftist, and "progressive" thinking from the 1960s. Expression counters repression; environmental degradation battles economic advancement. Old ways of making a living, such as mining, manufacturing, and military bases fade out, while continued agricultural production, and the boom of quality wine and electronic products remind all of California's innovativeness. War often gives purpose to domestic activity, exemplified in unity during World War II and divisiveness in Vietnam. California youth creatively rages against the preceding generation, while vibrancy, born in the Gold Rush, inspires risk-taking. Al Jolson sang in 1924, *California, Here I Come!* Sixty years later, the surfin' Beach Boys crooned, *California Callin'.* Why is this call so seductive? The answer lies with the title of a 1922 promotional pamphlet, "California: Where Life is Better." As proof, Hollywood-produced movies and television shows portray California as American essence writ large for the world to view.

Suggestions for Further Reading

GENERAL

Aker, Raymond and Edward Von der Porten. *Discovering Francis Drake's California Harbor*. Palo Alto, CA: Drake Navigators Guild, 2000.

Austin, Mary. *Land of Little Rain*. Boston: Houghton Mifflin, 1903. Extensively reprinted.

Bailey, Lynn R. *Supplying the Mining World: The Mining Equipment Manufacturers of San Francisco*. Tucson, AZ: Westernlore Press, 1996.

Bain, David H. *Empire Express: Building the First Transcontinental Railroad*. New York: Viking, 1999.

Boessenecker, John. *Gold Dust and Gunsmoke: Tales of Gold Rush Outlaws, Gunfighters, Lawmen, and Vigilantes*. New York: Wiley, 1999.

Clappe, Louise. *The Shirley Letters: Being Letters Written in 1851–1852 from the California Mines*. Marlene Smith-Baranzini, editor. Berkeley: Heyday Books, 1998.

Clark, William B. *Gold Districts of California*. Bulletin 193. Sacramento: California Division of Mines and Geology, 1970.

Coburn, Jesse L. *Letters of Gold: California Postal History through 1869.* Canton, OH: The U.S. Philatelic Classics Society, Inc., 1984.

Dana, Richard Henry. *Two Years Before the Mast.* New York: Harper, 1840. Extensively reprinted.

Daniel, Cletus E. *Bitter Harvest: A History of California Farm Workers, 1870–1941.* Ithaca: Cornell University Press, 1981.

Delgado, James P. *To California by Sea.* Columbia, SC: University of South Carolina Press, 1990.

Downey, Lynn. *This is a Pair of Levi's Jeans.* San Francisco: Levi Strauss & Co. Publishing, 1995.

Dunitz, Robert J. and James Prighoff. *Painting the Towns: Murals of California.* Los Angeles: RJD Enterprises, 1997.

Ferlinghetti, Lawrence and Nancy J. Peters. *Literary San Francisco.* San Francisco: City Lights Books, 1980.

Franks, Kenny A. and Paul F. Lambert. *Early California Oil: A Photographic History, 1865–1940.* College Station: Texas A&M University Press, 1985.

Harris, David. *Eadweard Muybridge and the Photographic Panorama of San Francisco, 1850–1880.* Montreal: Canadian Centre for Architecture, 1993.

Hart, James D. *A Compendium to California,* 2nd. ed. rev. Berkeley: University of California Press, 1987.

Hine, Robert V. *California's Utopian Colonies.* San Marino, CA: The Henry E. Huntington Library, 1953.

Holliday, J. S. *The World Rushed In: The California Gold Rush Experience.* New York: Simon & Schuster, 1981.

Hundley, Norris. *The Great Thirst: Californians and Water—A History.* 1992. rev. ed. Berkeley: University of California Press, 2001.

Jones, Holway R. *John Muir and the Sierra Club: The Battle for Yosemite.* San Francisco: Sierra Club, 1965.

Kelley, Robert L. *Gold vs. Grain: The Hydraulic Mining Controversy in California's Sacramento Valley.* Glendale: The Arthur H. Clark Company, 1959.

Kibbey, Mead B. *The Railroad Photographs of Alfred A. Hart, Artist.* Sacramento: The California State Library Foundation, 1996.

Kurutz, K. D. and Gary F. Kurutz. *California Calls You: The Art of Promoting the Golden State, 1870–1940.* Sausalito, CA: Windgate Press, 2000.

Moody, Ralph. *Stagecoach West.* New York: Thomas Y. Crowell Company, 1967.

Morse, Edgar W., ed. *Silver in the Golden State.* Oakland: The Oakland Museum History Department, 1986.

Muir, John. *The Mountains of California.* 1894. New York: Dorset Press, 1988.

Muscatine, Doris. *Old San Francisco.* New York: G. P. Putnam's Sons, 1975.

Orsi, Richard J. and John F. Burns, eds. *Taming the Elephant: Politics, Government, and Law in Pioneer California.* Berkeley: University of California Press, 2003.

Orsi, Richard J. and Ramón Gutiérrez, eds. *Contested Eden: California Before the Gold Rush.* 1997. Berkeley: University of California Press, 1998.

Orsi, Richard J and James J. Rawles, eds. *A Golden State: Mining and Economic Development in Gold Rush California.* Berkeley: University of California Press, 1998.

Orsi, Richard J., Kevin Starr, and Anthony Kirk-Greene, eds. *Rooted in Barbarous Soil: People, Culture, and Community in Gold Rush California.* Berkeley: University of California Press, 2000.

Paul, Rodman W. *California Gold: The Beginning of Mining in the Far West.* 1947. Lincoln, NE: University of Nebraska Press, 1965.

Powell, Lawrence Clark. *California Classics.* Los Angeles: The Ward Ritchie Press, 1971.

Robinson, Mary Judith. *From Gold Rush to Millennium, 150 Years of the Episcopal Diocese of California, 1849–2000.* San Francisco: The Episcopal Diocese, 2001.

Schneider, Jimmie. *Quicksilver: The Complete History of Santa Clara County's New Almaden Mine.* San Jose, CA: Zella Schneider, 1992.

Schrepfer, Susan R. *The Fight to Save the Redwoods.* Madison, WI: The University of Wisconsin Press, 1983.

Secrest, William B. *Lawmen & Desperadoes, 1850–1990.* Spokane, WA: The Arthur H. Clark Company, 1994.

Stadtman, Verne A. *The University of California, 1868–1968.* New York: McGraw-Hill, 1970.

Starr, Kevin. *Americans and the California Dream, 1850–1915; Inventing the Dream: California Through the Progressive Era; Material Dreams: Southern California through the 1920s; Endangered Dreams: The Great Depression in California; The Dream Endures: California Enters the 1940s; Embattled Dreams: California in War and Peace, 1940-1950.* Oxford: Oxford University Press, 1973, 1985, 1990, 1996, 1997, 2002.

Stoddard, Tom. *Jazz on the Barbary Coast.* 1982. Berkeley: Heyday Books, 1998.

Sunset Magazine. *The California Missions: A Pictorial History.* Menlo Park, CA: Lane Publishing Company, 1964.

Teiser, Ruth and Catherine Harroun. *Winemaking in California.* New York: McGraw-Hill, 1983.

Wagner, Jack R. *Gold Mines of California.* Berkeley: Howell-North, 1970.

Walker, Franklin. *A Literary History of Southern California.* Berkeley: University of California Press, 1950.

———. *San Francisco's Literary Frontier*. 1939. Seattle: University of Washington Press, 1969.

Wiltsee, Ernest A. *Gold Rush Steamers*. San Francisco: The Grabhorn Press, 1938.

PEOPLE

Agresti, Olivia R. *David Lubin: A Study in Political Idealism*. Berkeley: University of California Press, 1941.

Bagley, Will, ed. *Scoundrel's Tale: The Samuel Brannan Papers*. Spokane, WA: Arthur H. Clark Company, 1999.

Bonadio, Felice A. *A.P. Giannini: Banker of America*. Berkeley: University of California Press, 1994.

Caughey, John Walton. *Hubert Howe Bancroft: Historian of the West*. Berkeley: University of California Press, 1946.

Dillon, Richard H. *Iron Men: California's Industrial Pioneers, Peter, James, and Michael Donahue*. Point Richmond, CA: Candela Press, 1984.

———. *Wells Fargo Detective: A Biography of James B. Hume*. New York: Coward-McCann, Inc., 1969.

Drury, William. *Norton I: Emperor of the United States*. New York: Dodd, Mead & Company, 1986.

Egan, Ferol. *Frémont: Explorer for a Restless Nation*. 1977. Reno: University of Nevada Press, 1985.

Hildebrand, George H. *Borax Pioneer: Francis Marion Smith*. San Diego: Howell-North Books, 1982.

Kroninger, Robert H. *Sarah [Hill] and the Senator [William Sharon]*. Berkeley: Howell-North, 1964.

Lavender, David. *Nothing Seemed Impossible: William C. Ralston and Early San Francisco*. Palo Alto, CA: American West Publishing Company, 1975.

235

Leider, Emily Wortis. *California's Daughter, Gertrude Atherton and Her Times.* Stanford: Stanford University Press, 1991.

Lewis, Oscar. *George Davidson: Pioneer West Coast Scientist.* Berkeley: University of California Press, 1954.

Lower, Richard C. *A Bloc of One: The Political Career of Hiram W. Johnson.* Stanford: Stanford University Press, 1993.

Lyman. George D. *John Marsh, Pioneer.* New York: Charles Scribner's Sons, 1931.

McGinty, Brian. *Strong Wine: The Life and Legend of Agoston Haraszthy.* Stanford: Stanford University Press, 1998.

Monzingo, Robert. *Thomas Starr King: Eminent Californian, Civil War Statesman, Unitarian Minister.* Pacific Gove, CA: The Boxwood Press, 1991.

Nickel, Douglas R. *Carleton Watkins: The Art of Perception.* San Francisco Museum of Modern Art, 1999.

Rhodehamel, Josephine DeWitt and Raymund Francis Wood. *Ina Coolbrith: Librarian and Laureate of California.* Provo, UT: Brigham Young University Press, 1973.

Robinson, Judith. *"You're in Your Mother's Arms": The Life and Legacy of Congressman Phil Burton.* San Francisco: Mary Judith Robinson, 1994.

Scharlach, Bernice. *Big Alma: San Francisco's Alma Spreckels.* San Francisco: Scottwall Associates, 1990.

Solnit, Rebecca. *River of Shadows: Eadweard Muybridge and the Technological Wild West.* New York: Viking, 2003.

Tutorow, Norman E. *Life and Legacy of Leland Stanford, A California Colossus.* Spokane, WA: The Arthur H. Clark Company, 2004.

Walsh, James P. *San Francisco's [Vincent] Hallinan: Toughest Lawyer in Town.* Novato, CA: Presidio Press, 1982.

Williams, David A. *David C. Broderick: A Political Portrait.* San Marino, CA: The Huntington Library, 1969.

POPULATION

Burchell, R. A. *The San Francisco Irish, 1848–1880*. Berkeley: University of California Press, 1980.

Chan, Sucheng. *This Bittersweet Soil: The Chinese in California Agriculture, 1860–1910*. Berkeley: University of California Press, 1986.

Chinn, Thomas W. *Bridging the Pacific: San Francisco Chinatown and its People*. San Francisco: Chinese Historical Society of America, 1989.

de Graaf, Lawrence B., Kevin Mulroy, and Quintard Taylor, eds. *Seeking El Dorado: African Americans in California*. Seattle: University of Washington Press, 2001.

Gumina, Deanna Paoli. *The Italians of San Francisco, 1850–1930*. New York: Center for Migration Studies, 1978.

Houston, Jeanne Wakatsuki and James D. Houston. *Farewell to Manzanar*. Boston: Houghton Mifflin, 1973.

Jackson, Helen Hunt. *Ramona*. 1884. *The Annotated Ramona*, Antoinette May, ed. San Carlos, CA: Wide World Publishing, 1989.

Kroeber, Theodora. *Ishi in Two Worlds*. Berkeley: University of California Press, 1965.

Lapp, Rudolph M. *Blacks in Gold Rush California*. (New Haven, CT: Yale University Press, 1977.

Lee, Anthony W. *Picturing Chinatown: Art and Orientalism in San Francisco*. Berkeley: University of California Press, 2001.

Levinson, Robert E. *The Jews in the California Gold Rush*. New York: Ktav Publishing House, Inc., 1978.

Levy, Jo Ann. *They Saw the Elephant: Women in the California Gold Rush*. Hamden, CT: Archon Books, 1990.

Margolin, Malcolm. *The Ohlone Way: Indian Life in the San Francisco-Monterey Bay Area*. Berkeley: Heyday Books, 1978.

McClain, Charles J. *In Search of Equality: The Chinese Struggle against Discrimination in Nineteenth-Century America.* Berkeley: University of California Press, 1994.

Pitt, Leonard. *The Decline of the Californios: A Social History of the Spanish-Speaking Californians, 1846–1890.* Berkeley: University of California Press, 1966.

Stryker, Susan and Jim Van Buskirk. *Gay by the Bay.* San Francisco: Chronicle Books, 1996.

Takaki, Ronald. *Strangers from a Different Shore: A History of Asian Americans.* Boston: Little Brown and Company, 1989.

Index